D1388155

LAND
WINDOW TAX
ASSESSMENTS

Jeremy Gibson, Mervyn Medlycott
and Dennis Mills

Second Edition

Federation of Family History Societies

First published 1993 by the **Federation of Family History Societies.**

Second edition published 1998 by
Federation of Family History Societies (Publications) Ltd.,
2-4 Killer Street, Ramsbottom, Bury, Lancs. BL0 9BZ, England.

Copyright © Federation of Family History Societies, 1993, 1998,
on behalf of the editors, Jeremy Gibson, Sir Mervyn Medlycott, bt., and Dennis Mills.

This Guide incorporates and revises *Land Tax Assessments, c.1690 - c.1950,*
ed. Jeremy Gibson and Dennis Mills, F.F.H.S., 1983.

ISBN 1 86006 054 4

Typing by Elizabeth Hampson, computer typesetting in Arial and layout by Jeremy Gibson.
Printed by Parchment (Oxford) Limited.

Acknowledgments: *To the contributors to 'Land Tax Assessments', 1983*
The Editors would like to express their gratitude to all archivists and other record office staff who have assisted directly or indirectly in the preparation of this Guide. More particularly they wish to place on record and (themselves apart) thank those who compiled the county returns:
Dr Sarah Banks (Cumberland, Durham); W.T. Barnes (National Library of Wales: Breconshire, Cardiganshire, Montgomeryshire, Radnorshire); Dr. John Beckett (Nottinghamshire); Miss Susan Blay (Cheshire); Dr John Broad (Hertfordshire, London and Middlesex); Mrs Janice Capewell (Shropshire); Duncan Chalmers (Public Record Office); Mrs Mary Clements (Herefordshire); C.R.H. Cooper (Guildhall Library); Mrs Jan Crowther (Yorks. East Riding); Mrs Jean Dunn (Staffordshire); Michael Farr (Warwickshire Record Office); Norman Gardner (Lancashire, Westmorland); Jeremy Gibson (Oxfordshire); Peter Grey (Bedfordshire); Richard Grover (Hampshire, Kent, Surrey, Sussex); Stephen Harrison (Suffolk); Michael Havinden (Devon, Somerset); Ms Jennifer Hofmann (Dorset Record Office); Mrs Elizabeth Howard (Worcestershire); Dr Michael Jubb (Public Record Office); Professor Eric Kerridge (Merioneth); Dr Dennis Mills (Cambridgeshire, Huntingdonshire, Lincolnshire, Wiltshire); Dr Jeanette Neeson (Northamptonshire); Derek Palgrave (Yorks. West Riding, Doncaster); Ms Gwenith Parry (Llangefni Area Office, Gwynedd Archives Service: Anglesey); Miss Maureen Patch (Dyfed Archives Service: Carmarthenshire, Pembrokeshire); Simon Pawley (Leicestershire); Dr Rees Pryce (Montgomeryshire); Philip Riden (Glamorgan, Monmouthshire); Dr Bill Sheils (Borthwick Institute of Historical Research: Yorks. North Riding and York); Miss Joan Sinar (Derbyshire Record Office); Dr Kate Tiller (Berkshire); Dr Michael Turner (Buckinghamshire); Dr Robert Unwin (Yorks. West Riding); A.G. Veysey (Clwyd Record Office: Denbighshire, Flintshire); Miss Eleanor Vollans (Cornwall, Gloucestershire, Essex); G. Haulfryn Williams (Caernarfon Record Office, Gwynedd Archives Service); Ms Marion Laidler Wilson (Northumberland); Dr Richard Wilson (Norfolk).

To those who have helped since 1983 and with new material in this Guide:
Contributors to *Land Tax Assessments* have not been asked to revise their entries, but over the years archivists and others have sent us further information and corrections, and, as always, we are most grateful for these.
In the search for Window Tax records we have met similar assistance, and it would be invidious to single out specific repositories. We would, however, in addition, like to thank Roger Bellingham, for information about Selby records, and Anthony Camp and Susan Gibbons, for their description of the index to the Male Servants Tax, 1780, in the library of Society of Genealogists.

Federation of Family History Societies (Publications) Ltd. is a wholly owned subsidiary of
The Federation of Family History Societies, Registered Charity No. 1038721.

CONTENTS

INTRODUCTION

THE LAND TAX

by Dennis Mills

What was the Land Tax ?

The Land Tax was introduced in the late seventeenth century and was only finally abolished in the mid-twentieth. Its value to family historians (and indeed many others) is that it lists, year by year, the names of the proprietors of land in each parish and also, in theory, the names of the actual occupiers. It also can give some indication of the economic standing of those named.

For the major part of the two and a half centuries of its existence, the survival of the tax lists, county by county, division by division, and parish by parish, has been varying and fortuitous. Only for the period 1780 to 1832 is there any uniformity in their survival, when 'duplicates' are to be found for all or most of these years in the Quarter Sessions records of many counties, now in county record offices. From 1772 returns had been altered to incorporate a list of all occupiers of land in each parish (not necessarily shown earlier). From 1745 in principle, but from 1780 in practice, payment of land tax on freehold property worth two pounds or more annually established voting qualification, hence the records with the Clerks of the Peace. The only entirely uniform record is for the year 1798, for almost the whole of England and Wales, contained in 121 volumes in Class IR.23 at the Public Record Office, Kew.

The land tax is generally considered to date from the Act of 1692, 4 William and Mary, c.1, which was designed, like the 1671 subsidy and the aids of 1688, to tax personal estate, public offices and land. Assessments for the aids of 1688-9 survive for Hertfordshire and Nottinghamshire and others may appear in general collections of taxation documents. Early land tax assessments (hereafter LTAs) are similarly often found in collections with poll tax returns and/or local rate assessments, suggesting administrative links between the different forms of taxation.

After a few years of experiment it was decided in 1698 that the land tax should be levied on the so-called assessment principle. Instead of the Revenue taking one or two shillings in the pound of personal wealth, as in the subsidy principle, the assessment principle was based on a fixed sum which the government wished to levy from the country as a whole. This had the advantage that they knew in advance the theor-etical yield of the tax. The government gave counties assessments which it left them to share out between hundreds or wapentakes, where a similar division of responsibility occurred between the constituent parishes and townships. Once made in 1698, the switch to the assessment principle became permanent and county quotas remained fixed for the life of the tax, down into the nineteenth century (and in a modified form beyond). Variations in parish quotas were rare and only achieved by negotiation between neighbouring parishes. For administrative convenience, local assessors tended to avoid assessing items of wealth other than landed property and the annual legislation from 1702 became known as the Land Tax Act. Nevertheless the LTAs do sometimes, especially before 1798, contain a sprinkling of assessments based on the salaries of public offices (especially the hated excise officers) and on the stock-in-trade of urban merchants.

For its first ninety years, as this Guide shows, survivals of LTAs are comparatively rare, with few counties having complete runs even for single years. The most complete survival rate appears to be for the City of London, but in many counties there is virtually nothing. For the years following 1832, when reform of the franchise obviated the need for Land Tax duplicates to be collected or retained in Quarter Sessions records, survival again varies, mainly depending upon Land Tax Commissioners' deposits in county record offices. To most, their usefulness from 1832 is anyway much lessened. Since 1798 landowners had been able to redeem the tax. Though for voting purposes their names remained on record until 1832, thereafter they could be omitted. Therefore, one should expect declining numbers of names until 1949, when compulsory redemption was introduced. The tax was finally abolished in 1963 [Unwin, 1982].

What information do the LTAs contain ?

As common printed forms for LTAs were used after 1798, a description of their layout will give an indication of the information one can expect. Working from left to right the columns are headed as follows:-

1. **Rentals.** This column is often left blank, but where it has been completed the yearly values of the respective properties can be discovered and comparisons made elsewhere in the parish. In most parts of the country no systematic revaluation of properties was ever made after 1698, with the consequence that both rentals and assessments get progressively out of step with the real economy, especially in the urban and industrial areas. It is unwise, therefore, to lay any emphasis on the actual level of these figures, but a rough comparison with other properties in the same parish will give an approximate idea of your ancestor's standing in the parish (but remember that he may have had property in more than one parish).

2. **Names or proprietors and copyholders.** This column is generally reliable, though long term lessees and copyholders, rather than owners proper, may appear in it and one should watch for evidence that the entry is not quite up-to-date (e.g. cross check with burial registers). The adjective 'late' before a surname may indicate a recent death or the sale of the property. Titles such as Sir, Rev., Dr., Mr. and Esq., are used. Smaller property owners were sometimes omitted, especially perhaps in the lightly taxed northern counties.

3. **Names of occupiers.** Those with labouring ancestors may be disappointed here, since rows of cottages are often entered as 'Wm. Smith and others', while small tenancies of agricultural land may have suffered the same fate. Initials and Christian names do not always appear in this column, so caution is required, especially with frequently recurring names. Where 'ditto' occurs in this column it might occasionally mean owner occupation, rather than the same occupier as on the previous line, i.e. one should make as certain as possible that the ditto was not being used horizontally, rather than the vertical convention.

4. **Names or description of Estates or Property** (generally not in use until 1825/6). 'House and Land' accounts for a very large proportion of entries here, but more specific descriptions, such as mill, shop, workshop, inn (with the name) may appear. Before 1798 personal wealth and the nature of public offices are sometimes given, but the wealth figures cannot be treated as reliable. In parishes with more than one settlement, the names of village, hamlet, etc., may appear here, or those of individual large properties, but street names are rare.

5 and 6. **Sums assessed and exonerated; Sums assessed and not exonerated.** Sums assessed are the amounts of tax levied and, like the rentals, are not so important individually as when compared with each other. As the level of tax varied, one should note this as a problem when doing a chronological analysis. However, between 1772 and 1909 the rate remained at four shillings in the pound, so this precaution is only necessary with early assessments. In 1798 owners of properties valued under 20 shillings a year ceased to be chargeable but many had escaped taxation at earlier dates.

The term 'exonerated' here refers to the fact that, under the same act of 1798, it was possible to settle permanently with the Land Tax Commissioners in return for a commutation payment equivalent to 15 years' tax. (The 1798 Act in fact allowed both redemption by owners and purchase of the tax by third parties. Redemption, leading to exoneration from the tax, could be purchased before March 1799 by landowners buying 3 per cent consols yielding an annuity exceeding the tax by one-fifth. The huge increase in the price of consols in 1800 and 1801 made these terms very unfavourable, and in 1802 saw the first of many changes in them). Nevertheless, because LTAs were used until 1832 by the Clerks of the Peace as the basis for deciding electoral rights, it was necessary to record every substantial piece of property, whether actually taxed or not.

In some counties this style of form continued in use long after 1832, but most LTAs after this date contain only partial lists of owners and occupiers sometimes rather out-of-date, owing to the discontinuance of the electoral use to which they had been put before 1832. As mentioned above, in 1949 redemption became compulsory on property changing hands, and in 1963 all unredeemed land tax was abolished, but no records beyond 1948 have been released by the Inland Revenue.

Before the standardised forms of 1798 came into use one can expect less information in LTAs, and a greater degree of ambiguity concerning the standing of those whose names appear. Especially before c.1780, there is frequently only one set of names - are these the names of owners or of occupiers? Occupiers' names sometimes appear as internal evidence bears out, probably because they were the men on the spot from whom the tax could be collected. Where they were tenants they could have recouped these payments from their landlords in the form of rent rebates. However, except when there is evidence to the contrary, where a single column of names appears the historian should assume this to contain only proprietors' names, including lessees with long terms and copyhold tenants.

To sum up so far, the LTAs are most plentiful in the very period when parish registers are becoming less reliable, but before civil registration has begun and the first census enumerators' books have been compiled. The following summary of entries for a single property between 1780 and 1832 demonstrates the type of information such a study can yield.

Land Tax Assessments for the property now known as
Jasmine Cottage, High Street, North Collingham, Notts.

Dates	Name of Proprietor	Occupier	Description	Sum Assessed £. s. d.
1780, 1782-83	Widow DRING	Self	-	0. 2. 7.
1784-86	do	John BLAND	-	0. 2. 7.
1787-93	John DRING	Self	-	0. 2. 7.
1793	do	do	-	0. 0. 7.
1794	do	do	-	0. 1. 0.
1795-96	Dring's Trustees	John BIGGS	-	0. 0.10.
1797-1805	do	Joseph BIGGS	-	0. 0.10.
1806	do	WEST and others	-	0. 0.10.
1807	do	Jane TRICKET	-	0. 0.10.
1808-11	do	Wm. WEST and others	-	0. 0.10.
1812	do	Geo. TRICKET	-	0. 0.10.
1813	do	WEST and others	-	0. 0.10.
1815-23	Wm. WEST	Self	-	0. 0. 7.
1824-27	do	do	-	0. 1. 2.
1828-32	do	do	House and garden	0. 1. 2.

Notes
1. The rental is never given.
2. The LTAs for 1781 and 1785 are missing.
3. The property was identified with the help of the deeds, which start with William WEST, butcher, being admitted to the copyhold tenancy on 19 May 1814, when John and Mary ATKINSON were said to be the owner-occupiers.
4. At the time of the enclosure award in 1790 Elizabeth DRING was the owner and the area was 2 roods and 7 perches. Variations in assessment could be associated with the ownership of land away from the house, as well as real revisions of assessment.
5. Fractions of pennies have been omitted from the *Sum Assessed*.

Some points about using information from LTAs

The fortunate family historian may find a run of several decades of surviving LTAs, with perhaps the odd year missing here and there as we have seen in the Nottinghamshire illustration. Therefore, LTAs might be used in parallel with a series of registers, or as a partial substitute. Tracing the same name, or an heir, whether as owner, occupier, or both is not without some difficulties, although in principle it is simple enough. In the first place, most names appearing in a tax list are those of male heads of households, but they appear there isolated from their wives and children, so there is more risk than with register entries, that you have got the 'wrong man'. Only occasionally, in any single tax list, will there be clues as to linkage, e.g. 'self and son' appearing in the occupier column, or the description 'wife of X.Y.' for a female proprietor, or the terms 'junior' and 'senior'. When widows remarried their properties may appear under the names of their new husbands. Clergy were frequently owners by virtue of being incumbents, so changes in clerical names do not always, or even usually, have the same implications as for lay names.

Where John Smith has been assessed at £1.2s.6d. tax for a period of twenty or thirty years and is suddenly replaced by William Smith at the same amount, one can at least suspect that there was a relationship between the two. A careful consideration of the other entries on the LTAs for the changeover period will eliminate some of the doubt. For example, that parcel may have been the only property taxed at £1.2s.6d. Then the position on the form may act as a clue, since many assessors used a non-alphabetical order of names, which may relate in some way to the mode of collection. On the other hand, matters might not be as straightforward as in this example. John Smith's land may have been split between two or more heirs. In these circumstances one should not necessarily expect the new joint assessments to add up to the old assessment. John Smith may, of course, be followed by another John Smith, without the indicators senior and junior!

Nevertheless a run of assessments often makes things clearer to the family historian. For example, in the Cambridgeshire parish of Melbourn the Tithe Survey of 1839 shows that Joseph CAMPKIN, who owned 50 acres of arable land and nearly two dozen tenements, curiously did not live in his own house. Instead, he was occupying the house, shop and warehouse belonging to John CAMPKIN, while John lived in one of Joseph's houses! Such an arrangement suggests family connections, but the Campkins were staunch nonconformists, so clues in the registers are insufficient to the task. The riddle was solved by studying the LTAs carefully from 1810 onwards. A John CAMPKIN is holding property as early as 1810, but this cannot be the first John, since the censuses give his date of birth as c.1810. Joseph first appears in 1820 as an owner occupier, but from 1826 is also renting a house from John senior, which formerly John himself was using. John senior was buried in 1833 and in 1834 the young John appears in the LTA in his place, there referred to as Joseph's son; while an earlier assessment has referred to Joseph as the older John's son. So at last the three generations are linked. This unusual reference to such relationships in any LTA may be explained by the fact that Joseph Campkin himself was a Melbourn land tax assessor and collector from 1815 to 1851 and his father served in that capacity at least in 1810. Nevertheless this example shows some of the possibilities and the care with which one must handle them. It was, incidentally, quite usual for the assessors to appoint themselves as collectors of the tax and not uncommon to find that the same people were also overseers of the poor and, therefore, the principal rate collectors in the parish. The collector received poundage, whilst the office of assessor was unpaid.

Finally it is worth remembering that, in addition to many non-resident owners, taxpayers may not have lived in the parishes even where they occupied property, since it was not unusual for farms to have land in two parishes, or for shopkeepers to live away from their shops, while woodland was often 'occupied' by members of the gentry whose mansions were many miles away.

How are the collections of LTAs arranged?

The answer to this question relates to the various ways in which the documents were brought together in the past, as well as the various arrangements of convenience which have been adopted by different archivists. In this guide we have adopted a division into three periods, namely **pre-1780, 1780-1832**, and **post-1832**, since before the survey was undertaken it seemed to accord with conventional wisdom, based on the 'fact' that the middle period was distinguished by virtue of the LTAs having doubled as electoral registers. A good deal of variation from the tripartite division has been found to exist in a significant number of record offices, though not enough to cause us to depart from it.

When the subject of the land tax is mentioned, most archivists think in terms of:

1. The land tax duplicates lodged c.1780-1832 with the Clerks of the Peace in their capacity as what we would now call electoral registration officers;
2. Those deposited by the Commissioners of Land and Assessed Taxes (Inland Revenue Collectors' Offices) in the period after 1832; and
3. Other deposits, not all of which will come to mind immediately, because land tax documents are often only one of many types of documents within these deposits. The Clerks of the Peace, or Quarter Sessions records do, however, often figure again in the pre-1780 period.

There are at least three reasons why one should expect some LTAs of the pre-1780 period to appear in Quarter Sessions' records. In their Historical Association booklet H-62, *County Records*, F.G. Emmison and I. Gray point out that it was enacted as early as 1745 'that no person could claim to vote unless assessed to the land tax'. This Act represents an early attempt to set up a system which did not finally materialise for the whole country until 1780, when a further, more effective Act was passed. This will help to explain why in some counties sporadic survivals began about 1745 and gather momentum in the 1770s and why pre-1780 LTAs are sometimes to be found in the same collections as, and are catalogued with, the survivals of 1780-1832. It may not be too big a stretch on the imagination to suggest that the 1780 Act arose out of the good practice of a number of progressive counties, since this is a characteristically English (British) way of introducing change, as in the fields of police, poor law, education and sanitary reform. A second reason is that Clerks of the Peace, as Emmison and Gray demonstrate, were responsible for enrolling, registering and generally looking after a very wide range of documents, so that stray collections might have gravitated towards their offices for this reason alone. Thirdly, Clerks were solicitors in practice on their own account and therefore handled many deeds and collections of estate papers, including those of gentlemen who acted as land tax commissioners, or were commissioners themselves.

In addition to these deposits in county record offices, there is a uniform country wide record for 1798 (only) in the Public Record Office, Kew, Class IR.23. As described on page 6, from 1798 land-owners were able to redeem the liability for the annual tax by a single lump sum payment, known as exoneration. Consequently there was a need for a record of all land owners and occupiers, and the result is a series of 121 volumes giving this information for this year. Normally these give no details of the properties listed, and sub-tenants and sharing tenants are not shown. In some towns householders may be listed by street (e.g. Abingdon, Berks.) but in others no such differentiation is made (e.g. Banbury, Oxon). It has even been noticed that despite pages being allowed for a place and headed with its name, they have been left blank (e.g. Bath, Somerset) (the editors would be grateful for information on similar lacunae). The most surprising omission is the entire county of Flint, though in this case there is just no volume nor reference for it. In such cases the Parish Books of Redemptions, Class IR.22, should supply information on those exonerating land. The IR.23 registers themselves provide the date of exoneration and a cross-reference to the full contract in Class IR.24. Although these contracts are fairly verbose, they add little to the details in IR.23; but they should give the acreage held, and in the case of exoneration some time after 1798, may show intervening changes in ownership.

The exact volume number references for Class IR.23 have been shown under the individual county sections. The P.R.O. class list in a footnote remarks that some volumes contain assessment details for other years, showing dates of 1799 to 1801 against entries. Such post-1798 assessments are only for occasional parishes; the nationwide assessment relates solely to 1798 itself.

The importance of this nationwide coverage is obvious, particularly in the cases of Berkshire, Cornwall, Rutland, Shropshire and several of the Welsh counties, where locally held county series do not survive; and for boroughs where the LTAs are often missing. For a debate on the econometric use and misuse of the P.R.O. series see the numbers of *Economic History Review* for February 1981 (vol. **34)** and August 1982 (vol. **35**).

To sum up, then, in the period before 1780 one might find the LTAs in Quarter Sessions records, in estate and family archives, and even occasionally in parish deposits where the parish assessors', rather than the commissioners' clerks' copies have survived. Between 1780 and 1832 we are largely served by the Quarter Sessions (or Clerks of the Peace) collections, but there are again exceptions, and a few areas possess two sets of copies which have arrived at record offices by different routes. There is also the important record of 1798 LTAs in Class IR.23 in the Public Record Office, for some counties the only record to survive. In the third period again, there is some overlap to be expected. While survivals in estate and parish records are unusual, the Inland Revenue deposits are sometimes supplemented by Quarter Sessions collections running on beyond 1832.

Using the Land Tax Assessments

Now, some practical suggestions as to how your search can be prosecuted. First, **make an appointment with the record office**, stating that you would like to look at the land tax assessments for the parish of X over a period of, say, 25 years on either side of a given date. Such a statement can be supplemented by information given in this Guide. If the LTAs are bundled by parish there should be few problems, since such a request will probably only require one or two boxes to be produced. However, when the LTAs are bound together in annual volumes for a county or division, one cannot expect 50 large tomes to be produced. Some other means of searching will have to be devised, such as asking for half a dozen volumes spread over a 30 year period. The nature of your existing knowledge will obviously determine your strategy.

There may also be the problem of knowing in which Hundred or other division your parish was located. County directories and other guides in search rooms will usually give the requisite information. Once this has been discovered our Guide will be of greater value to you, but bear in mind the possibility that your parish may be one of those for which LTAs have been lost, despite a good survival rate in the Hundred more generally.

We have followed the pre-1974 boundaries in compiling this Guide, as these will generally accord with the geographical limits of collections of LTAs, but this is not an invariable rule. For example in East and West Sussex archives follow modern, rather than historical boundaries, while the Hampshire Record Office continues to contain LTAs for areas administered since 1974 by Dorset and the Isle of Wight County Councils.

In some counties, e.g. the new Cambridgeshire, and Wiltshire, more detailed handlists have been compiled and printed and we quote these where known. Other similar findings lists are available in a typewritten form in record offices, e.g. Anglesey. Where we have given full references, especially to LTAs within estate and parish deposits, it will be helpful to give the archivists this information.

Those family historians whose ancestors lived in cities which were also counties (e.g. Lincoln, York) may already be familiar with the special circumstances of the archival collections of these places. The survival rate of LTAs in urban areas generally is nowhere as high as for rural areas, since the 40s. freeholders were not a feature of most urban parliamentary constituencies. Especially in the south of England, boroughs could be quite minor settlements. Nevertheless they were responsible for their own tax administration, with the result that their tax records are to be found in borough archives rather than Quarter Sessions collections. In major cities with a tradition of care for archives, such as London and Bristol, much more complete LTA records may be found. In any case, many other lists of householders were available in towns, especially those of freemen and burgesses, and ratebooks have probably survived on a more comprehensive scale. It is to these kind of documents that the family historian should turn for information comparable to that given in the LTAs in the counties.

A note on the history of landownership and the use of the LTAs by historians

There is a very large literature on the history of landownership, which it would be impossible to summarise here, but room can be spared to mention a few leading authorities. Still basic to the subject are the studies of large estates published by Gordon Mingay and F.M.L. Thompson in 1963. Other useful works by Mingay are those of 1976, 1981, and 1990, to be found in the list at the end of this Introduction.

Historians have used the LTAs themselves for two main purposes: to trace the supposed decline in the small landowner, and to construct typologies of rural communities. The debate about the small landowner started for political as well as academic reasons in the first decade of the present century and has gone on intermittently ever since. Useful summaries are available in Ginter, 1991 and 1992; and in Turner and Mills, 1986.

The basic problem is that the LTAs are riddled with inaccuracies that make it impossible to convert amounts of tax paid into acreages held on a consistently accurate basis. There was also the tendency for the very smallest owners to be brought in or left out of the tax base in order to balance the books to achieve the quotas fixed in 1698. Within these rigid quotas there is not enough evidence for historians to have a clear view of what were probably widely differing practices from one parish to another. For example, in mining districts the circumstances differed sharply from those where fen drainage had increased the rental values of land several fold. In any case, returning to the small landowner, there is now something of a consensus that the crucial decline occurred in centuries before the land tax appeared.

Nevertheless, many small properties did survive into the land tax era, many of them concentrated in particular districts, eg, the south west of England, rather than the midlands and East Anglia, and in particular villages. Almost anywhere in England, estate (closed) villages dominated by a single large proprietor can be found, whilst within a few miles there will often be 'open' villages divided between several scores of owners of varying importance. It is relatively easy to recognise polar opposites, like Tysoe and Compton Wynyates in Warwickshire (Ashby 1961), quite another matter to classify all parishes occupying the continuum between the extremes.

Yet our ancestors would easily have recognised the different atmospheres of lordless villages and estate villages, those where every aspect of life seemed to swing round the character and whims of the estate owner. The present writer has been keen to distinguish between the estate 'system' and the 'peasant' system (especially in Mills, 1980) and to trace their competing influences through rural communities. There is relatively little difficulty with the idea of the estate system, except that some criticis do not readily accept that some estate owners varied from the norm without destroying it. The essential idea is that they were powerful enough to please themselves whether they tolerated nonconformists and public houses, or got rid of them; whether they rode to hounds or spent their leisure in the serious pursuit of art, and so on.

Much more controversial is the use of the term 'peasant' in a nineteenth century English context, when literate contemporaries often used the word pejoratively, or to refer to the landless labourer. This is quite the opposite to my own view that we should reserve the term to indicate men who were independent cultivators of the soil, sometimes owning land of their own, a cut above the unfortunate labourers, from whose ranks they had often dragged themselves. Marxist historians have been especially hostile to this concept, largely because the term 'peasant' has a different and politically self-conscious use in their literature (Reed and Wells, 1990).

Recently, Ginter (1991, 1992) has introduced a better understanding of the appropriate uses of the LTAs, in brief demonstrating the dangers of using them to study long term trends, but supporting them as a means of classifying rural communities. A number of interesting case studies have been published since my review of the latter subject in 1980. For example, in her study of parts of Berkshire and Norfolk, Banks (1988) has shown how complex were the statistical relationships which I had perhaps oversimplified. In the context of the Lincolnshire Wolds, Rawding (1991) has explored the ways in which major landowners, such as the Earl of Yarborough, expressed their power over the countryside, and sometimes restrained themselves from doing so. The open-closed model probably suits arable areas of England well because there the need for large armies of harvest workers was great, inducing wide differences in population between the closed villages of the estate owners and the open villages of the peasantry and other less grand proprietors. This idea has been supported by Bell (1990), who has shown that the model does not help so much in understanding rural communities in a more pastoral and industrialised county like Staffordshire.

Note. Grateful acknowledgment is made to the Open University Faculty of Social Sciences for funds in assistance of photocopying. We would also like to acknowledge the help of a number of colleagues, archivists and friends in preparing this introduction, including John Beckett, the late Terrick FitzHugh, Richard Grover, Philip Riden, Michael Turner and Peter Walne. They are not, however, to take any responsibility for our errors! We invite interested parties to send notes for addition or amendment to us at Harts Cottage, Church Hanborough, Witney, Oxon. OX8 8AB.

WINDOW AND OTHER ASSESSED TAXES

by Mervyn Medlycott

Not so many records of the Window and Other Assessed Taxes survive as for the Land Tax, mainly because few were filed in Quarter Sessions records for electoral purposes. However, the material located in our survey forms a most useful addition to land tax coverage, particularly for counties and boroughs without Quarter Sessions Land Tax holdings, and for Scotland. The extensive Scottish collection in central government records at the Scottish Record Office for the period 1748 to 1802 is of particular value, in a country with few land tax holdings.

Fortunately the window and other assessed taxes are easier to explain in their essential details than the land tax. Complexity will however arise if researchers attempt to link window tax entries to houses marked on maps or still standing in house history studies, as rarely were all windows in a house liable to tax. Windows in certain service rooms, such as dairies, and shops and business premises attached to dwellings, were at various times exempted from tax, but rules on such exemptions were constantly being changed, so it is difficult to work out in any particular year which windows were liable to tax and which were not. However, sudden changes in numbers of windows, for people in those places fortunate enough to possess long runs of annual assessments, presumably indicate when buildings were being extended, reduced, rebuilt or indeed newly built. It may even be possible to ascertain thereby the year that a dwelling was erected. The potential of window taxes for house history studies has so far been under-utilised, probably because few knew what assessments existed.

The Window Tax was introduced in 1696 (7 and 8 William III, c.18), being recast in new acts in 1747 and 1797, and was repealed in 1851. There were various intervening renewing and amending acts, but these, for most practical purposes, should be ignored. It was in fact two taxes in one: the *house tax*, assessed on the actual occupiers of inhabited dwellings which were liable to church and poor rates, on which there was a flat rate charge, further overlaid in 1778 with an additional charge based upon rateable values; and the *window tax*, another additional charge for which there was a graduated scale of bands on houses with more than a certain number of windows, being ten or more between 1696 and 1766, seven or more 1766-1825, and eight or more 1825-1851. Rather oddly the house tax was repealed in 1834, but the window tax on dwellings with eight or more windows remained on the statute books for a further seventeen years. Some assessments, such as those in the Sussex Q.S. records, are for the window tax alone. Others will include the house tax element as a standard tax charge but will omit to state the numbers of windows for dwellings with fewer than ten, seven or eight in relevent periods. The Scottish series often give window numbers for smaller dwellings even though below window tax liability. This may have been an administrative convenience if at any time these dwellings were extended, thus becoming liable.

Generally fewer names will be given for the window tax than for the land tax, and no more than might already appear in parish ratebooks. Usually the only details given are the taxpayer's name, number of windows and tax payable. It should be observed that the vast majority of taxpayers named actually lived in the dwellings for which they were assessed. There is none of the confusion which can arise in the land taxes of 'occupiers' who did not live in the place in which they appear (as mentioned by Dennis Mills on page 8). Status of taxpayers can be compared in the window tax from numbers of windows given, as they can from land valuations in the land tax.

The most notorious aspects of window taxes were the many loopholes which existed for tax evasion. Window openings could be blocked permanently or temporarily, with some form of camouflage removed after the assessor had done his work. An even simpler form of evasion arose out of the exemptions allowed on service and business premises attached to dwellings. A bit of furniture moving and a bribe offered to the assessor could reduce an individual's charge substantially. Successive governments tried to prevent these abuses, rendering the tax more and more complex to administer. The fact that it constantly failed to raise the revenue required of it is testament to the resourcefulness of the British in outwitting the taxman, and led eventually to seeking revenue from other sources - land holding for example could not be disguised in the way that houses and windows could.

After 1784 window and house tax assessments were consolidated with what are known as the 'assessed taxes' - such as on shops, male and female servants, horses, carriages, carts and waggons, and hair powder - and these were administered together on the same assessment forms. These could provide considerable information on taxpayers lives, stating whether they had shop premises, if they employed servants, how many horses that had, even whether they used hair powder, had a fob watch or claimed a coat of arms. Mr Roger Bellingham tells us that some Selby, Yorkshire, assessments give the occupations of those who paid tax on shop premises. We hope this may apply to other places too. Some of these taxes were disastrous in their consequences and remained on the statute books for very short periods, most notably the clock and watch tax, repealed within a year in 1798, and the female servants tax, which created distortions on the labour market, and was applied for only seven years, 1785-92. Yet other forms of taxation worked well, at least from the point of view of governments raising revenue, such as Income Tax, introduced in 1798, still very much with us.

Prior to 1784 these various taxes were assessed separately. Very few assessments survive that early, apart from some window and house taxes, though there are the national series at the Public Record Office, Kew, for carriage duties, 1753-66, on (gold and silver) plate duties, 1756-62, and male servants tax for 1780. The P.R.O. references for these are: *Carriage Duties*, 1753-1766: T.47/2-4; *Plate Duties*, 1756-1762: T.47/5; *Male Servants Tax*, 1780: T.47/8, and they are described and illustrated by Dowell (1884) and more recently by Stella Colwell (1991).

The **Society of Genealogists** holds an Index to those paying the tax on *Male Servants, 1780*. This is in nine small volumes on the State Papers shelves. Within each initial letter this is arranged by county, and, except for London and Westminster (where streets are given), no further location. Surnames are often prefaced 'Mr' without initial. The London, Middlesex and Hertfordshire sections were published in *Middlesex and Hertfordshire Notes and Queries*.

Colwell also mentions that some levies of duties or taxes 'are traceable among receipts of surcharges imposed on defaulters, the county bundles of dated scraps of paper giving their names and addresses and penalties' in Class E.182. Before eager researchers attempt to examine E.182 they should be warned that it is a gigantic class, and the annual county bundles, comprising scores of separate pieces, are completely unsorted, promising nothing but dirt and frustration, with very little likelihood of the discovery of any really relevant material!

References and Bibliography

ASHBY, M.K. (1961), *Joseph Ashby of Tysoe, 1859-1919*, Cambridge University Press.

BANKS, Sarah (1988), 'Nineteenth-century scandal or twentieth-century model?: a new look at "open" and "close" parishes', *Economic History Review*, **41**, pp.51-73.

BARNES, F.A. (1982), 'Land tenure, landscape and population in Cemlyn, Anglesey', *Transactions of the Anglesey Antiquarian Society and Field Club*, 1982, pp.15-90.

BECKETT, J.V. (1976), 'Local custom and the "New Taxation" in the 17th and 18th centuries', *Northern History*, **12**, pp.105-26.

BECKETT, J.V. (1980), *Local taxation: national legislation and the problems of enforcement*, Standing Conference for Local History, 1980.

BECKETT, J.V. (1982), 'The decline of the small landowner in the 18th and 19th century England: some regional considerations', *Agricultural History Review*, **30**, pp.97-111.

BECKETT, J.V. (1985), 'Land Tax or Excise: the levying of taxation in 17th and 18th century England', *English Historical Review*, **100**, 395, pp.285-308.

BELL, David J. (1990), *Open and close parishes in nineteenth century Staffordshire: testing the causal thesis*, Department of Geography, Staffordshire Polytechnic, Occasional Paper **14**.

BRITISH PARLIAMENTARY PAPERS (1844), *Land Tax redeemed and unredeemed in England and Wales (HC 619)* **XXXII**. 389. This contains a complete list of land tax divisions and parishes for 1798 and the quotas for which they were assessed.

COLWELL, Stella (1991), *Family roots: discovering the past in the Public Record Office*, Weidenfeld and Nicolson, pp.63-64, 157 (demonstrating practical use, for family historians, of LTAs in IR.23 and IR.24, and of other assessed taxes in T.47).

COLWELL, Stella (1992), *Dictionary of genealogical sources in the Public Record Office*, Weidenfeld and Nicolson, p.110.

DAVEY, R. (ed.) (1991), *East Sussex Land Tax 1785*, Sussex Record Society, **77**.

DOWELL, Stephen (1884), *Taxation and taxes in England* (reprinted 1988), also reprinted with illustrations of actual assessments by Malcolm Pinhorn in *Blackmansbury*, **3**.3/4, 5/6, **4**.1-4 (1966-67).

EMMISON, F.G. and GRAY, I. (1961), *County records*, Historical Association booklet H-62, with later revisions and reprints. The 1987 revision omits the Appendix listing Land Tax holdings in record offices.

GINTER, D.E. (1991), 'Measuring the decline of the small landowner', in HOLDERNESS, B.A. and TURNER, M. (eds.), *Land, labour and agriculture, 1700-1920: essays for Gordon Mingay*, Hambledon Press.

GINTER, Donald E. (1992), *A measure of wealth: the English land tax in historical analysis*, Hambledon Press.

JOHNSON, A.H. (1909), *The disappearance of the small landowner*, Oxford University Press, reprinted Merlin Press, 1963.

HOLDERNESS, B.A. (1972), '"Open" and "close" parishes in England in the 18th and 19th centuries', *Agricultural History Review*, **20**, pp.126-39.

LANGTON, J. (1979), *Geographical change and industrial revolution: coalmining in south-west Lancashire, 1590-1799*, Cambridge University Press (especially Appendix 4: Land Tax Assessments Returns as a source of Colliery Data).

MARTIN, J.M. (1979), 'The small landowners and parliamentary enclosure in Warwickshire', *Economic History Review*, **32**, pp. 328-43.

MEDLYCOTT, Mervyn (1993), 'The Window Tax: a survey of holdings in Britain', *Genealogists' Magazine*, **24**.5 (pp.186-89) (the content of which is, by permission, included in this Guide).

MILLS, D.R. (1980), *Lord and peasant in nineteenth century Britain*, Croom Helm.

MILLS, D.R. (1982), 'The significance of the land tax assessments', *Local Historian*, **15**, pp.161-65 (Report of the 1981 conference which led to the survey summarized in this Guide).

MINGAY, G.E. (1963), *English landed society in the eighteenth century*, Routledge and Kegan Paul.

MINGAY, G.E. (1976), *The gentry, the rise and fall of a ruling class*, Longmans.

MINGAY, G.E. (1981), *The Victorian countryside*, 2 vols., Routledge and Kegan Paul.

MINGAY, G.E. (1990), *A social history of the English countryside*, Routledge.

MITCHELL, Ian (1981a), 'Pitt's Shop Tax in the History of Retailing', *The Local Historian*, **14**, 6, pp.348-351.

MITCHELL, S.I. (1981b), 'Retailing in 18th and early 19th century Cheshire', *Transactions of the Historic Society of Lancashire and Cheshire*, **130**, pp.37-60.

MITCHELL, Ian (1984), 'The development of urban retailing 1700-1815', in Clark, P. (ed.), *The Transformation of English Provincial Towns*,.

NOBLE, M. (1979), *Change in the small towns of the East Riding of Yorkshire c.1750-1850*, Hedon Local History Society, **5**.

NOBLE, M. (1982), 'Land tax returns and urban development', *Local Historian* **15**, pp.86-92.

RAWDING, Charles (1992), 'Society and place in nineteenth century north Lincolnshire', *Rural History*, **3**, pp. 59-85.

REED, Mick and WELLS, Roger (eds.) (1990), *Class, conflict and protest in the English countryside, 1700-1880*, Frank Cass. (Contains a very good bibliography.)

RIDEN, Philip (1987), *Record sources for local history*, Batsford (pp. 62-63).

SHEPPARD, June A. (1992), 'Small farms in a Sussex Weald Parish [Chiddingly], 1800-60', *Agricultural History Review*, **40** (II), pp.127-41.

STEPHENS, W.B. (1981), *Sources for English local history* (revised edition), Cambridge University Press, pp. 87-90.

THOMPSON, F.M.L. (1963), *English landed society in the nineteenth century*, Routledge and Kegan Paul.

TURNER, M.E., and MILLS, D.R. (eds.) (1986), *Land and property: The English Land Tax 1692-1832*, Alan Sutton, Gloucester.

UNWIN, R.W. (1982), *Search guide to the English Land Tax*, West Yorkshire County Record Office.

WEST, John (1997), *Village records* (3rd edn.), Phillimore.

WILSON, G.J. (1980), 'The land tax and West Derby Hundred 1780-1831', *Transactions of the Historic Society of Lancashire and Cheshire*, **129**, pp.63-91.

BEDFORDSHIRE

Land Tax

Bedfordshire Record Office, Bedford:

1) **Pre-1780:** *Manshead Hundred,* 1750, complete
[F 89];
a few isolated LTAs as below.
2) **1780-1832:** 1783 complete (except *Bedford*)
[HA 14/5];
1782-83 Bedford (town) [BOR B F/16/1-2];
1797-1832 [QDL], NC.
3) **Post-1832:** variable coverage according to
Hundred, arranged by place [LX series for long
runs; isolated returns have refs. as below].

LTAs are arranged by place.

Hundreds (for 1783, 1797-1832, see above):
Barford: 1) Great Barford, 1720, 1740, 1750, 1753,
1758 [FN 1253-4];
Renhold, 1697, 1706, 1717 [PO 14].
2) Renhold, 1782 [PO 14].
3) 1930-49, SY, MP;
Great Barford, 1901 [X 290/338];
Ravensden, 1841, 1865-6 [X 65/140-2];
Wilden, 1838 [P 106/28/2].
Biggleswade: 1) Biggleswade parish, 1765 [RI 1/3];
Old Warden, 1770 [PE 195].
3) 1915-49, MY, MP;
Biggleswade parish, 1841 [X 440/718];
Potton, 1899 [LX 83];
Sandy, 1891 [LX 91a];
Tempsford, 1869; 1874, 1884-5 [WY 911].
Clifton: 3) 1915-49, SY, MP.
Flitt: 1) Silsoe, 1750 [L 28/35].
3) 1857-1946, MY, MP.
Manshead: 1) 1750, NC [F 89].
3) 1834-1946, MY, MP.
Redbornstoke: 1) Ampthill, 1725, 1739-41
[R 4/319-20, Duke of Bedford estates];
Houghton Conquest, 1725 [R 4/318];
Maulden, 1765-6 [P 31/28/4].
3) 1842-1949, MY, MP.
Stodden: 1) Bolnhurst, 1750 [Fac 17/2];
Keysoe, 1765, 1767 [C 1722-3].
3) 1930-49, MY, MP.
Willey: 1) Felmersham, 1757 [V 292]; Radwell in
Felmersham, 1764 [V 293];
Podington, 1737, 1739, 1748, 1763 [OR 1752-7];
Thurleigh, 1765, 1767 [C 1722-3].
2) Podington, 1784-5 [OR 1760-1], 1787 [OR 949],
1789 [OR 1764].
3) 1930-49, MY, MP;
Farndish, 1883-87 SY [OR 950];
Podington, 1882-93 SY [OR 950].
Wixamtree: 3) 1917-49, MY, MP;
Northill, 1902 [LX 77].

Bedford (town): 2) 1782-3, 1797-1832.
3) 1930-49, SY, SP.

Public Record Office, Kew:
Whole *County,* 1798 [IR.23/1] (see page 9).

Window Tax

Bedfordshire Record Office, Bedford:

Keysoe, 1731 [P 48/28/1].
Great Barford, 1750-67 [FN 1253,1255].
Old Warden, 1770 [PE 196].

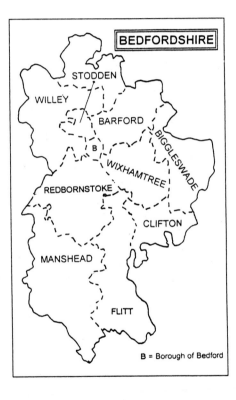

BEDFORDSHIRE

STODDEN
WILLEY
BARFORD
B
WIXAMTREE
BIGGLESWADE
REDBORNSTOKE
CLIFTON
MANSHEAD
FLITT

B = Borough of Bedford

LTA = Land Tax Assessment; M = Many; NC = Near Complete; P = Parishes; S = Some; Y = Years

BERKSHIRE

Berkshire Record Office, Reading:

No locally held official series of LTAs exists for the county since the papers of the Clerk of the Peace do not survive. The following list is therefore drawn from fragmentary examples found in parish records and collections of private papers in the B.R.O. It is possible that scattered copies for other parishes or townships may come to light in collections of papers not yet available to the public. No series of LTAs are known to survive in separate borough or city collections in the county.

The main survival is for 1716, in the Pleydell Estates Tax Book [BRO D/EP b E9] for the following places:

Ashbury, Barrington, Becket, Bourton, Buckland, Caswell, Charney, Compton, Great and Little Coxwell, Little Farringdon, Fernham, Hatford, Hinton, Inglesham, Kingston Lisle, Langford, Longcot, Longworth, Pusey, Shellingford, Shilton, Shrivenham (tything), Uffington, Watchford.

Survivals for other years as follows:
Abingdon: 1) 1773.
2) 1795-6.
Ashbury: 1) 1743.
Baulking (hamlet): 2) 1787-8, 1791-2.
Beedon: 1) 1745.
Binfield: 1) 1740, 1779.
Bourton: 1) 1728, 1732, 1740.
Brightwalton: 1) 1679-1767.
Burghfield: 2) 1789.
Buscot: 3) 1840, 1843.
Chaddleworth: 2) 1805.
Coleshill: 1) 1716, 1723, or 8(?), 1729, 1741.

Great Coxwell: 1) 1738-9, 1741, 1761.
Englefield: 2) 1778.
Fernham: 1) 1743.
Forest petty sessional division: 3) 1876-1919 NC [PS/FT 22] (for Arborfield-cum-Newland, Barkham, Binfield, Earley, Easthampstead, Finchampstead, Hinton, Ruscombe, Sandhurst, Sonning, Waltham St. Lawrence, Warfield, Wargrave, Whistley, Winnersh, Wokingham; also Wargrave 1920, and Finchampstead and Sandhurst 1921).
Kingston Lisle: 1) 1743.
West (or Great) Shefford: 1) 1740, 1743.
Shrivenham (tything): 1) 1718, 1723, 1727.
Stratfield Mortimer: 1) 1718, 1721 (2), 1724.
Sulham: 1) 1704, 1753, 1771.
Sutton Courteney: 3) 1866-7.
Uffington: 1) 1743.
Warfield: 3) 1846-75, 1922 (see also Forest p.s.).
Watchford: 1) 1704.
Woolhampton: 1) 1704.

Buckinghamshire Record Office, Aylesbury.
Windsor 1944-50; Maidenhead 1935-36, 1949-50 [7/5].

Public Record Office, Kew:.
Whole *County*, 1798 [IR.23/2] (see page 9); this constitutes the only full coverage of the county.

Window Tax

Berkshire Record Office, Reading:
Abingdon borough, 1752, 1753 [D/EP 7/166].
Englefield, 1778 [D/P 52/28/2].

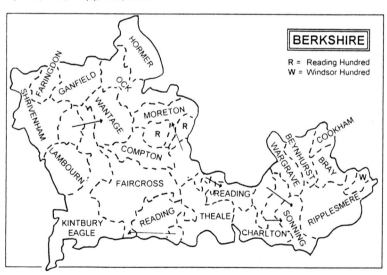

BERKSHIRE

R = Reading Hundred
W = Windsor Hundred

LTA = Land Tax Assessment; M = Many; NC = Near Complete; P = Parishes; S = Some; Y = Years
---

BUCKINGHAMSHIRE

Land Tax

Buckinghamshire Record Office, *Aylesbury:*

1) **Pre-1780:** 1753, *Cottesloe Hundred*; otherwise isolated survivals.
2) **1780-1832:** good coverage [Q/RPL/1-8]. Majority now available on microfilm.
3) **Post-1832:** C19/20, *Desborough, Newport Hundreds*; C20 *Burnham* and *Stoke Hundreds*.

LTAs are arranged by place.

Hundreds

Ashendon: 2) 1782-7, 1789, NC; 1790, SP; 1791, 1793-5, NC; 1796-7, SP; 1798-1802, 1804-32, NC.
Aylesbury: 1) Hartwell, 1777 [D/LE/17/10];
  2) 1780-1, SP; 1782-1832, NC.
Buckingham: 2) 1780, SP; 1782-93, NC; 1794, SP; 1795-1831, NC.
  N.B. There are a few records for Buckingham borough.
Burnham: 1) Amersham, 1765 [D/DR/12/88-92]; Chesham, 1718, 1738 [D/CH, uncatalogued, Box 6], 1743 [D/LO/70].
  2) 1783-1831, NC.
  3) 1935-49 [AR/33/64].
Cottesloe: 1) 1753, all parishes [Q/unclass./Q/50].
  2) 1782, two parishes; 1781-89, NC; 1790, SP; 1791-1832, NC.
Desborough: 1) West Wycombe, 1689, 1700, 1703, 1705, 1707, 1709, 1712 [PR/227/28/1].
  2) 1780-82, SP; 1783-96, NC; 1797, SP; 1798-1831, NC.
  3) 1832-70; 1900-01, 1905-06, 1910-11, 1915-16, 1920-21, 1925-26, 1930-31, 1936, 1940, 1942-43, 1946-47; Brands Fee only 1894-97 [AR/53/63]. LT redemption papers (incomplete) 1799-1946.
Newport: 2) 1780-1, SP; 1782-99, 1801-17, 1819-32, NC. Redemptions from 1799 [7/9].
  3) 1833-1922, 1925, 1928, 1930, 1935, MY, MP [AR/47/56]; LT redemption papers, 1799-1868.
Stoke: 1) Denham, 1773, 1776, 1780-81 [D/W/68/1-6].
  2) 1781-1821, 1823-32, NC.
  3) 1935-49 [AR/33/64].

Berkshire Record Office, *Reading:*
Wraysbury: 1) 1705 [D/ED E4B/2].

Oxfordshire Archives, *Oxford:*

Boycott: 2) 1786-92, 1794-1814, 1816-32.
Kingsey, Tythrop: 2) 1786-1832 MY.
Lillingstone Lovell: 1) 1760.
  2) 1786-92, 1794-1810,1812-4, 1816-32.

Public Record Office, *Kew:*
Whole *County*, 1798 [IR.23/3,4] (see page 9).

Window Tax

Buckinghamshire Record Office, *Aylesbury.*
Burnham Hd.: Chesham, 1798-99 [PR44].
Newport Hd.: 1797-1806.

Other Taxes

Newport Hd.: Income Tax 1879, 1882-83; Personal Tax 1833.

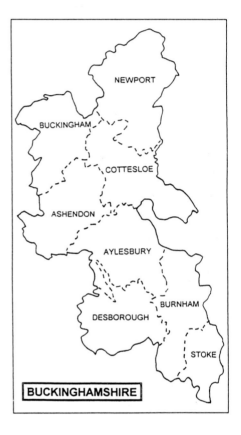

BUCKINGHAMSHIRE

LTA = Land Tax Assessment; M = Many; NC = Near Complete; P = Parishes; S = Some; Y = Years

CAMBRIDGESHIRE and the ISLE OF ELY

Land Tax

Cambridgeshire Record Office, Cambridge:

1) **Pre-1780:** Ely, South Witchford, 1750-79; Radfield South, Chilford, Whittlesford, 1759-63, otherwise isolated LTAs only.
2) **1780-1832:** Most of County, 1829-32; otherwise partial survivals.
3) **Post-1832:** varying C19/20 survivals.

LTAs are arranged by place except 1829-32; *Genealogical Sources in Cambridgeshire R.O.*, 2nd edn., 1994, gives years of surviving LTAs for each parish.

Hundreds
Cambridge (town): 2) 1829-32, Complete, but no LTAs for Stourbridge Fair or the University.
Radfield Northern half: 2) 1829-32, Complete.
   3) 1878-88, Complete.
Cheveley: as *Radfield N.* plus
   2) Newmarket 1801-7.
Staploe: as *Radfield N.* plus 2) Soham 1798.
Radfield Southern half: 1) 1759-63, NC.
   2) 1789-1832, Complete.
   3) 1833-1948, NC.
Chilford: as *Radfield S.* plus
   1) Linton, 1694.
Whittlesford: as *Radfield S.*
Thriplow: 2) 1810- or 1811-32, Complete.
   3) 1833-1948, NC.
Armingford: as *Thriplow* plus
   1) Meldreth, 1699-1720; and
   (1 & 2) Bassingbourn, 1715, 1722, 1728, 1795.
Chesterton: 2) 1829-32, Complete.
   3) 1880-1948, Complete.
Northstow: as *Chesterton.*
Papworth: 1) Elsworth, 1769.
   2) 1829-32, Complete; Over, 1790.
   3) 1880-1948, NC.
Wetherley: 1) Comberton, 1707; Coton, 1767; Orwell, 1736.
   2) 1829-32, Complete, plus scatter 1780-1828.
   3) 1833-1948, 1880-1948 or 1890-1948, Complete.
Longstow: 2) 1829-32, Complete.
   3) 1946-48, Complete.
Ely: 1) 1750-1779, Complete.
   2) 1780-1832, Complete.
   3) 1833-1948, Complete.
South Witchford: as *Ely.*
North Witchford: 1) Chatteris, 1755.
   2) Nil.
   3) 1934 or 1946-48.
Wisbech: 2) 1798-1803, SP.
   3) 1935-48, NC.

Public Record Office, Kew:
   Cambridgeshire, 1798 [IR.23/5]; *Isle of Ely,* 1798
   [IR.23/26] (see page 9).
   Microfilm at **Cambridgeshire Record Office.**

Window Tax

Cambridgeshire Record Office, Cambridge.

Ely, Trinity 1764, 1779 [297/034].
Mepal 1752, 1762-64, 1766-75, 1779-82 [297/08].
Newmarket, All Saints 1803 [R57/15B/21(c)].
Wentworth 1761-63 [297/013].

Suffolk Record Office, Bury St. Edmunds.
   Kennett 1782 [339/34].

CAMBRIDGESHIRE and the ISLE OF ELY

WISBECH

WHITTLESEY and THORNEY

NORTH WITCHFORD

ELY

SOUTH WITCHFORD

STAPLOE

PAPWORTH

NORTH CHESTERTON

STOW

STAINE

CHEVELEY

C

FLENDISH

LONGSTOW

WETHERLEY

THRIPLOW

RADFIELD

CHILFORD

ARMINGFORD

WHITTLESFORD

Sfk.

C = CAMBRIDGE Liberty

LTA = Land Tax Assessment; M = Many; NC = Near Complete; P = Parishes; S = Some; Y = Years

CHESHIRE

Land Tax

Cheshire Record Office, Chester:

Cheshire (excluding Chester, see below):
1) Pre-1780: Wirral only, 1778-9.
2) 1780-1832: good coverage (no 1788).
3) Post-1832: sparse survival.

LTAs from Quarter Sessions records are arranged by township [QDV 2 1-490], available on microfilm in their original form. All post-1832 LTAs are in the LT Commissioners' papers.

Hundreds
Broxton: 2) 1784-7, 1789-98, 1800, 1803-17, 1819-32, NC.
3) 1938.
Bucklow East: 2) 1780, 1784-7, 1789-1831, NC.
3) 1833-99, 1937-41.
Bucklow West: 2) as Bucklow East.
3) 1833-1946.
Eddisbury: 2) 1785-7, 1789-98, 1800, 1802-32, NC.
3) 1938.
Macclesfield (Prestbury div.):
2) 1784-7, 1789-1831, NC.
Macclesfield (Stockport div.):
1) 1703-18, SP, SY [Arderne papers].
2) 1780, 1784-7, 1789-97, 1799-1831, NC.
Nantwich: 2) 1781-7, 1789-99, 1802-32, NC.
3) 1897-9, 1938-9, 1947-49.
Northwich: 2) 1781-7, 1789-1831, NC.
3) 1938-49.
Wirral: 1) 1778-9, NC.
2) 1780-7, 1789-92, 1794-1803, 1805-32, NC.
3) 1929-31.

City Record Office, Chester:
Chester (city): 1) 1704 (whole city); 1764, 1767, 1769, SP;
2) 1787-92, 1794, 1796-8, SP.

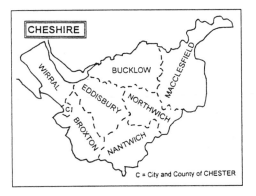

CHESHIRE

BUCKLOW
WIRRAL
EDDISBURY
MACCLESFIELD
NORTHWICH
C¹
BROXTON
NANTWICH

C = City and County of CHESTER

Warrington Library.
Penketh 1792-1858 [MS 2019].
Warrington 1782, 1793-1802, 1804 [MS 203-213; mf 47-48]; 1785 transcript [MS 1319, mf 71]; Woolston 1785-1815 transcript [p5301].
Assessed taxes (incl. Window Tax) 1790-1803 SY [MS 187-197, 218; mf 47-48].

Public Record Office, Kew:
Whole County, 1798 [IR.23/6,7] (see page 9).

Window Tax

Cheshire Record Office, Chester.
Chester, St. Mary 1779, 1781 [P20/26/8,9].
Halton 1771-74, 1809/10 [P10/23/11-15].

City Record Office, Chester.
Chester, St. Martin's and St. John's Ward, 1764; St Mary's, 1767; St. Michael's 1769 [CAS/2].
Chester (whole city) n.d. (c.1795-1806) [CAS/3] (1,500 names).

CORNWALL

Land Tax

Cornwall County Record Office, Truro:

It is essential that anyone wanting to consult archives in the R.O. first makes an appointment (phone 01872 273698/323127). Summer months are particularly busy. LT registers have been microfilmed, and enquirers will be constrained by the number of microfilm readers available.

The Record Office holds few parish LTAs prior to 1800. Those copies (period 2) which were deposited with the Clerk of the Peace are known to have been destroyed many years ago. But for 1798 see **Public Record Office,** page 22. Of the few isolated assessments which survive locally for period 1 and 2, several belong in large deposits of manorial records and other estate papers; some of these refer to farms and hamlets rather than parishes. Occasionally there are incorporated items such as poor rates which serve a comparable purpose in listing names and dues. As cataloguing of the deed collection continues, there may be additions to the small number of parishes at present named in the subject indexes under Land Tax.

1) **Pre-1780**
East Division: Landulph, 1742, Linkinhorne, 1710, 1736: Quethiock, 1753.
Powder West: Creed, 1709; Grampound, 1728, 1738, 1750-1, 1761-2.
Pyder: Crantock, 1725; Newlyn, 1763.
Padstow, 1734, 1739 [P170/18/3,4].
West Penwith: Gulval, LTAs and other papers from 1690 to 1830.

LTA = Land Tax Assessment; M = Many; NC = Near Complete; P = Parishes; S = Some; Y = Years

Cornwall *continued*

2a) Prior to 1800
East Division: Quethiock, 1788; St. Mellion, 1788.
East Penwith: Golant, 1794; St. Erth, 1797.
Lesnewth: Davidstow, 1795; Poundstock, 1795.
Powder East: Fowey, 1784.
Powder West: Gerrans, 1786; Grampound, 1798; Probus, 1787.
West Kerrier: Landewednack, 1780.
West Penwith: Gulval, see page 21.

2b) Early 19th century
'Register of land tax redemption contracts', compiled post-1805, and, of similar form 'Register of land tax redemption contracts', corrected to 1812 [AD 103/228,229].

In each register, the parishes of Cornwall are arranged in alphabetical order, and a list of contents given. The data for each parish are tabulated, and include the names of tenements, proprietors and occupiers. The Register corrected to 1812 is incomplete; there are blank pages headed by parish names, notably in the sections for names, beginning with L and S.

Owing to the loss of the LTAs of this period (apart from 1798, in *P.R.O.*, see right), the Registers are of unique importance and have been microfilmed, copy also at the *Society of Genealogists*.

2c) 1800-1832
For the post-1800 period a parish index for particular years of LTAs held has been compiled.

The only records which contain more than isolated survivals of LTAs are for *East Penwith* (1809-1875) and *West Kerrier* (1809-24) - a book of duplicates of sums assessed [193/58].

3a) Nineteenth century
Kerrier: 1834-on, MP; 1870-on, SP; some years missing.
Penwith: 1832-on SP (half); 1871-on, NC; some years missing.
Powder East: 1899, all.
Powder West: pre-1900, odd P, 1 or 2 Y.
Pyder: 1832-on, all P; some years missing.
Stratton: 1856, 1869, all P.
Trigg: 1899, MP.
West: 1830s-on, all P; some years missing.

See C.R. Sadler (1994), 'Patterns of Land Ownership and Occupation in Cornwall in the second half of the Nineteenth Century'. Cornwall County Record Office, Truro.

3b) Twentieth century
Records of all divisions comprise many years and nearly all parishes.

Public Record Office, Kew:
Whole *County*, 1798 [IR.23/8-11] (see page 9).

In view of the foregoing remarks under the County Record Office section, the P.R.O. holding is clearly of great importance.

Window Tax

Cornwall Record Office, Truro.

St. Dominic, 1766 [P50/28/2].
St. Erme, 1793-4, 1796-7, 1804-5 [P57/2/1].
Grampound, n.d., c.1750 [J 2068].
Gulval, 1777-8, n.d., c.1780, 1794-1800 [X173/28-56].
Lostwithiel, 1735 [B/LOS 371].
North Petherwin, 1717-8, 1725, 1728, 1796, 1802 [P167/28/5/1-4, and X355/239,243-44].

Port Eliot Muniments (private estate collection of the Earl of St. Germans, *Port Eliot, St. Germans,* from N.R.A. catalogue).
East hundred, 1770 [no. 541].

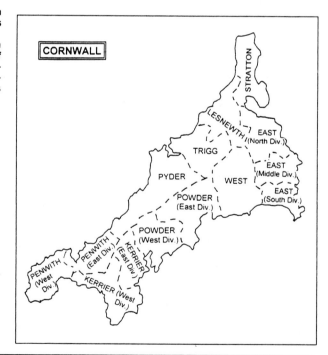

CORNWALL

LTA = Land Tax Assessment; M = Many; NC = Near Complete; P = Parishes; S = Some; Y = Years

CUMBERLAND

Land Tax

Cumbria Record Office, Carlisle:

1) **Pre-1780:** 1761 or 1762 for all wards except Leath [Earl of Lonsdale's papers]; later 1760s, most wards; 1770s, Allerdale Above, Cumberland wards [Quarter Sessions QRP 1].
2) **1780-1832:** good coverage [QRP 1].
3) **Post-1832:** some survivals.

LTAs from Quarter Sessions records 1764-1832 are arranged by townships. Complete list available. Post-1832 survivals have not been sorted, so dates given here are a rough guide only.

Wards
Allerdale Below:
1) 1762, NC; 1764, 1767, SP;
   1751, Scales; 1755, Woodside, Rosley, Bothill and Treaplow;
   1761, Sunderland;
   1768, Westnewton, Langrigg, Scales.
2) 1780-82, 1790-92, 1794, 1796, 1802, 1806-7, 1810, 1817-20, 1822-29, NC.
3) 1868-1949 SY, SP.
Allerdale Above: 1) 1762, 1767-70, 1772-3, 1775-8, NC;
   1766, Drigg and Castleton; 1779, MP.
2) 1780, 1782-3, 1785, 1787-9, 1791-4, 1796, 1804-8, 1817-29, NC;
   1781, SP; 1784, MP;
   1795, Kelton and Winder.
Cumberland: 1) 1761, 1766-70, 1779, NC;
   1764, 1777, MP;
   1762, Wigton, Blencogo, Kirkbride, High Sabersham;
   1771, Wiggonby, Blencogo, Carlisle Fisher St.;
   1772, Aglionby.
2) 1781-2, 1785, 1789-92, 1794, 1805, 1810, 1817-20, 1822-9, NC; 1784, MP.
3) 1845-1949, SY, SP.
Leath: 1) 1767-70, NC.
2) 1780, 1782-4, 1788-9, 1791-5, 1817-9, 1823-5, 1827-9, NC; 1785, MP.
Eskdale: 1) 1761, 1764, 1766, NC; 1767, MP.
2) 1780-6, 1788-96, 1810, 1817-20, 1822-1829, NC.
3) 1836-57, SY, SP.

Public Record Office, Kew:
Whole *County*, 1798 [IR.23/12,13] (see page 9).

Window Tax

Cumbria Record Office, Carlisle:

Egremont, 1761 [D/lec/240/Egrmt/Land Tax file].
Threlkeld, n.d., 18th century [SPC/21/20].
Thursby, 1805 [DX/1360], publ. in *Cumbria FHS Newsletter* no. 72 (Aug. 1994) pp. 22-23.
Whitehaven, 1770 [QRP/1, with land taxes].

DERBYSHIRE

Land Tax

Derbyshire Record Office, Matlock:

1) **Pre-1780:** High Peak Hundred, 1778-9; otherwise isolated survivals only.
2) **1780-1832:** practically complete, listed in detail and microfilmed, arranged by year.
3) **Post-1832:** C19 LTAs for two parish deposits. Some C20 survivals for many parishes, not listed in detail.

Wapentake or Hundred (periods 1 and 3, and period 2 additions to above):
Appletree: 1) Doveridge parish LTA, 1754 [D1197A/PW34].
3) None, unless included in the *Morleston and Litchurch* divisional records which have not been checked in detail.
High Peak: 1) 1778-9, NC;
   Monyash parish LTA, 1721 [D504 B/L439].
2) also Hope LTAs, 1798-1892 [D 1038-A/PT179-232].
3) 1935-49, SP [D162 and D243]; Hope, 1798-1892 (see above).
Morleston and Litchurch (the parishes in the former borough of Derby make individual returns):
2) see also redemption lists below.
3) 1799-1949, redemption registers [D233]; 1900-49, MP [D233]; 1930-49, SP [D244].

LTA = Land Tax Assessment; M = Many; NC = Near Complete; P = Parishes; S = Some; Y = Years

Derbyshire *continued*

Repton and Gresley: 3) 1919-47 redemption notices (also for West Goscote, Leics.) [D228T/A43]; 1936-49, LTA books [D228T/A1-42].

Scarsdale: 1) South Normanton parish LTA, 1755 [D37M/RE9].

Tipshelf parish LT returns, 1692-1702 [D1091 A/PO2] and LTA, 1700 [D1091 A/PO430].

3) 1940-6, duplicate LTAs for ten parishes in extreme N.E. [D244]; 1942-9, MP [D243]; Ashover, 1865-1911 [D59A/PZ44-78].

Wirksworth: 1) 1705-19, SY, SP [D258, Gell papers]

2) Dethick, Holloway, 1786 [D.1088M/R 9]. 1799-1835, SP, redemption lists [D243].

3) as above; and 1935-49, SP [D162 and D243]. Bonsall LTA, 1853 [D161 B/1/43].

Sheffield Archives
Bowden Chapel, 1722 [Bag C 331/2].
Staveley, 1719-20, 1751-54 [JC 1722-30], 1758 [JC 1842].

Public Record Office, *Kew:*
Whole *County,* 1798 [IR.23/14,15] (see page 9).

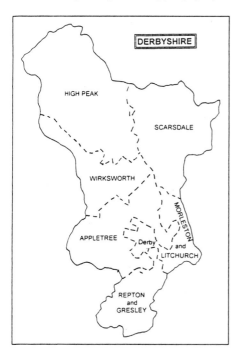

DERBYSHIRE

HIGH PEAK

SCARSDALE

WIRKSWORTH

MORLESTON

APPLETREE

Derby and LITCHURCH

REPTON and GRESLEY

Window Tax

Derbyshire Record Office, Matlock:
Denby, 1763, 1770, 1771, 1777 [D1428A/PO 24-7].
Dethick, 1786 [D1088M/R9].
Hathersage, 1713-4, 1717, 1719, 1765, 1769 [D1970A/ 'Window Tax'].
Hope, 1801-03, 1807/8, 1815-40 [D1038A/PT 30-34, 92-93].

Sheffield Archives.
Hasland 1811-12 [Bag C 575/4].
Staveley 1758 [JC 1731].

DEVON

Land Tax

Devon Record Office, Exeter:

1) **Pre-1780:** 1747, 1751, *Coleridge, Stanborough Hundreds; Exeter,* isolated LTAs. Otherwise pre-1780 LTAs have not been listed below; though numerous they are not catalogued under Hundreds, but under individual parishes, in D.R.O. index of LTAs.

2) **1780-1832:** good coverage. Full catalogues under Hundreds and by parish, under 'Quarter sessions' and 'Exeter Borough'. LTAs are arranged by place.

3) **Post 1832:** LTAs, though numerous, are catalogued only by parish (see D.R.O. index of LTAs) rather than Hundred, and have not been listed below. Later LTAs run up to 1952.

Hundreds
Axminster: 2) 1780-1832, NC.
Bampton: 2) 1780-1832, NC.
Barnstaple Borough: 2) 1780, 1782-3, 1785, 1787-8, 1790-1, 1795-9, 1801-32.
Braunton: 2) 1780-1832, NC.
Budleigh, East: 2) 1780-1832, NC.
Budleigh, West: 2) 1782, 1788-1832, NC.
Cliston: 2) 1780-1832, NC.
Coleridge: 1) 1747, 1751, NC.
2) 1780-1832, NC.
Colyton: 2) 1780-1832, NC.
Crediton: 2) 1780, 1782-1832, NC.
Ermington: 2) 1780-1832, NC.
Exeter City: 1) 1730, 1739, 1740-3, 1746-1751, 1755-7, 1767.
2) 1798-1825, LT redemptions only.
3) 1833-55, miscellaneous records.
Exminster: 2) 1780-5, 1787-1832, NC.
Fremington: 2) 1780-1832, NC.
Halberton: 2) 1780-2, 1787, 1789-90, 1792, 1794-1832, NC.
Hartland: 2) 1780-6, 1789-90, 1793-1832, NC.
Hayridge: 2) 1780-7, 1789-90, 1792-1832, NC.
Haytor: 2) 1780, 1782-5, 1787-1831, NC.
Hemyock: 2) 1780-3, 1785, 1788-1832, NC.

LTA = Land Tax Assessment; M = Many; NC = Near Complete; P = Parishes; S = Some; Y = Years

Devon continued

Lifton: 2) 1780-4, 1786-90, 1792, 1794-1832, NC.
South Molton: 2) 1780-4, 1787-90, 1792-1832, NC.
Ottery St. Mary: 2) 1780, 1782, 1788-9, 1791, 1793-1796, 1798-1832, NC.
Plympton: 2) 1780-95, 1797-1832, NC.
Roborough: 2) 1780-6, 1788-1832, NC.
Plymouth Borough: 2) 1780-1831, SY, SP (most from 1812 only;
St. Andrew's and Charles wards, 1826-31 only;
Old Town ward 1st div., 1812-15 only).
1 & 3) See **Plymouth and West Devon R.O.**
Shebbear: 2) 1780-1832, NC.
Shirwell: 2) 1780, 1782-6, 1789, 1791-1832, NC.
Stanborough: 1) 1747, 1751, NC.
2) 1780-4, 1786-90, 1792-1832, NC.
Tavistock: 2) 1780, 1782-5, 1788-90, 1792-1832, NC.
North Tawton and Winkleigh: 2) 1780-1808, 1810-1832, NC.
Teignbridge: 2) 1780, 1782-1831, NC.
Tiverton: 2) 1780-3, 1788-1832, NC.
Black Torrington: 2) 1780-4, 1787-1832, NC.
Witheridge: 2) 1780-1832, NC.
Wonford: 2) 1780-1832, NC (includes Exeter St. Leonard and St. Thomas).

Plymouth and West Devon Record Office:

Plymouth Borough: 1) Miscellaneous LTAs (few).
2) See above, **Devon R.O.**, *Exeter.*
3) Miscellaneous LTAs, 1831-1949.

Public Record Office, *Kew:*
Whole *County,* 1798 [IR.23/16-19];
City of Exeter, 1798 [IR.23/20] (see page 9).

Society of Genealogists:
South-West Devon, 1780. Computer print-out.

Key to Map of Devon Hundreds

14	Axminster	20	Haytor
9	Bampton	13	Hemyock
28	Black Torrington	27	Lifton
1	Braunton	3	South Molton
17	East Budleigh	16	Ottery St. Mary
6	West Budleigh	24	Plympton
11	Cliston	25	Roborough
21	Coleridge	30	Shebbear
15	Colyton	2	Shirwell
5	Crediton	22	Stanborough
23	Ermington	26	Tavistock
E	Exeter	29	North Tawton
18	Exminster		and Winkleigh
32	Fremington	19	Teignbridge
8	Halberton	7	Tiverton
31	Hartland	4	Witheridge
12	Hayridge	10	Wonford

Window Tax

Devon Record Office, *Exeter:*

West Alvington, 1773-91 [818A/PZ 16-44].
Buckland Tout Saints, 1787, 1790-93 [818A/PZ 79-83].
Cadbury, Cadeleigh and Nether Exe, 1710 [326M/Z 2-4].
Exeter, Allhallows on the Walls, St Olave, 1740-41;
St. Stephen and Bedford Precinct, 1756; St. Martin 1768-69 [D3 159f G1]
Halberton, 1710 [1160M/Parish/|General 4].
Mamhead, 1788 [4056M/0 1].
Manaton, 1755 [75/3/6].

North Devon Record Office, *Barnstaple:*

Hartland, 1816 [1201A/PW 7 and PO 751].
Meshaw, 1754 [1794A add/PW2].
Northam, 1781-82 [1843A/PD 12].

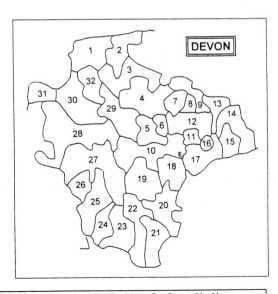

LTA = Land Tax Assessment; M = Many; NC = Near Complete; P = Parishes; S = Some; Y = Years

DORSET

Public Record Office, Kew:
Whole *County*, 1798 [IR.23/21,22] (see page 9).

Land Tax

Dorset Record Office, Dorchester:

The Dorset R.O. has good coverage of the whole county (except Poole) for 1780-1832, arranged by place, but very little for other periods.

1) **Pre-1780:** Alton Pancras 1715, 1738.
2) **1780-1832:** all divisions of the pre-1974 county, excluding Poole, NC.
3) **Post-1832:** Poole 1894-1927; *Bridport Division*, 1833-1946; *Wimborne Division*, 1931-46; collectors' duplicates 1924-35.

Window Tax

Dorset Record Office, Dorchester:
Edmondsham 1760 [Ph 774].
Evershot, 1785 [QDE(L):54/6/6].

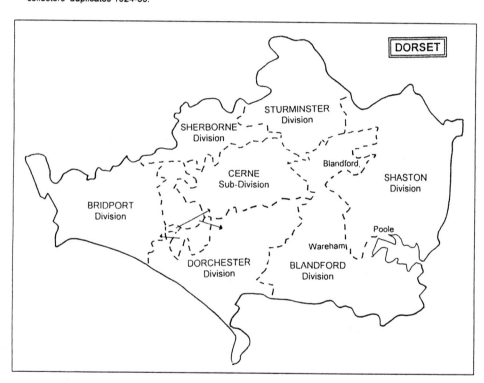

DORSET

STURMINSTER Division

SHERBORNE Division

CERNE Sub-Division

Blandford

SHASTON Division

BRIDPORT Division

Poole

Wareham

DORCHESTER Division

BLANDFORD Division

Note. There are over fifty hundreds and liberties in Dorset, many of them comprising only a very few parishes or even just one. For administrative purposes these areas were grouped in Divisions, as shown on this map. As the 1780-1832 LTAs are arranged by place, rather than hundreds and liberties, no attempt has been made to create a map showing these,

LTA = Land Tax Assessment; M = Many; NC = Near Complete; P = Parishes; S = Some; Y = Years

DURHAM

Land Tax

Durham County Record Office, Durham:
Durham University Library Archives and Special Collections, Durham.

1) **Pre-1780:** 1759-61, all wards have virtually complete sets of LTAs for at least one of the years;
1769, *Bedlingtonshire;*
1770, *Norham and Islandshire.*
2) **1780-1832:** good coverage.
3) **Post-1832:** late C19 and/or C20 for several wards.

There are two separate collections of LTAs for County Durham which duplicate and supplement each other. The *County Record Office* collection [Q/D/L] covers only the periods 1 and 2, arranged by year, whilst the collection held by the *University of Durham* covers all three periods, arranged by place. Catalogues to both collections are available. Prior enquiry should be made to establish in which collection any particular LTA may be.

Division
Bedlingtonshire: 1) 1760-1, 1769, NC.
  2) 1788-9, 1795, 1797-8, 1802-3, 1810-4, 1817, 1823-8, NC.
Chester East: 1) 1759-61, NC.
  2) 1795, 1797-8, 1802-3, NC;
  1810-4, 1820-1, 1826-7, 1829-31, MP;
  1788-9, 1817-9, 1823-4, 1828, SP.
  3) 1858-1949, MY, MP.
Chester Middle: 1) 1759-61, NC.
  2) 1789, 1795, 1798, 1802-4, 1810-4, 1817, 1819-1828, NC; 1829-31, MY, MP.
  3) 1858-1949, MY, MP.
Chester West: 1) 1759-61, NC.
  2) 1788-9, 1797-8, 1802-3, 1810, 1813, 1817, 1819, 1821, 1824-5, NC;
  1812, 1814, 1820, 1823, 1826-31, MP; 1811, SP.
  3) 1858-1949, MY, MP.
Darlington North West: 1) 1759-60, NC.
  2) 1783, 1785, 1787-9, 1803, 1810, 1812, 1817, 1823-4, 1826-8 NC; 1802, 1811, 1829-31, SP.
  3) 1899-1949, MY, MP.
Darlington South East: 1) 1759-61, NC.
  2) 1783, 1789, 1802-3, 1810-2, 1817, 1821-24, 1826-7, 1831-2, NC; 1828-30, SP.
  3) 1911-49, MY, MP.
Darlington South West: 1) 1759-60, NC.
  2) 1783-6, 1788-9, 1802-3, 1806-7, 1810, 1812,1815-7, 1822-8, NC; 1811, 1829-31, SP.
  3) 1911-49, MY, MP.
Easington North: 1) 1760, NC.
  2) 1785, 1787-91, 1793, 1795-6, 1798-1832, NC.
  3) 1833-1914, 1934-49, MY, MP.

Easington South: 1) 1759-60, NC.
  2) 1785, 1787-93, 1795-1832, NC.
  3) 1833-1914, 1933-49, MY, MP.
Norham and Islandshire: 1) 1759-66, NC;
  1760, 1770, MP.
  2) 1817, 1819-20, 1826-8 NC; 1788-9, 1823-4, MP; 1822, SP.
  3) See Northumberland, page 47.
Stockton North East: 1) 1759, NC;
  1735, 1744 for Elwick Hall [Salvin Papers, DRO D/Sa E/844-46].
  2) 1784-5, 1788-9, 1791-3, 1801-2, 1806-7, 1810, 1812, 1814-5, 1818-9, 1822-8, NC;
  1811, 1817, MP; 1798, SP.
  3) 1933-49, MY, MP.
Stockton South West: 1) 1759, NC.
  2) 1785, 1788-9,1791, 1793, 1801-2, 1806, 1810, 1812-9, 1821-9, NC; 1803-4, MP; 1830, SP.
  3) 1833-49, MY, SP.

Public Record Office, Kew:
  Whole *County*, 1798 [IR.23/23-25] (see page 9).
  Palatinate (?whole county), 1812-13 [DURH 3/199]; 1823-24 [DURH 3/200-01].

Inhabited House Tax (incl. windows)

Durham County Record Office
  Easington Ward, 1795-96 [Q/D/LM/1-26] (650 names).

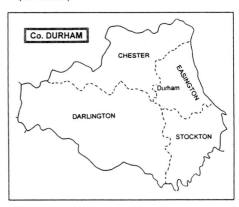

Note. For Norham and Islandshire, and for Bedlingtonshire, see the map of Northumberland on page 47.

LTA = Land Tax Assessment; M = Many; NC = Near Complete; P = Parishes; S = Some; Y = Years

ESSEX

Land Tax

Essex Record Office, Chelmsford:

1) **Pre-1780:** 1698, Becontree, Chafford, Havering;
1762-79, Freshwell, Hinckford, MY;
otherwise isolated LTAs only.
2) **1780-1832:** good coverage (Havering from 1794
only) [Quarter Sessions, Q/RP1].
Arranged by year.
3) **Post-1832:** sporadic survivals [from Commissioners
of Land and Assessed Taxes papers, D/Z 2].

Information in the *Guide to the Essex Record
Office* (E.R.O. **51**, revised to 1969) is abstracted in
the listing below. Isolated LTAs among parish
records, not listed here, appear in the *Catalogue of
Essex Parish Records 1240-1894* (E.R.O. **7**, 2nd
(revised) edition, 1966).

Of outstanding importance is the slip index to
20,000 personal names in the LTA of 1782, available at the E.R.O.

The post-1832 returns for *Dengie, Epping* and
Walden divisions, asterisked right, are stored away
from County Hall at Old Court, Arbour Lane, and
can only be viewed there, by prior appointment, at
present time normally on a Wednesday.

Hundreds

Barstable: 2) 1781-1832, NC.
Becontree: 1) 1698, Complete [D/DMs 027/1-28].
2) 1780-1832, NC.
3) SY, SP.
Chafford: 1) 1698, Complete [D/DMs 027/1-28].
2) 1781-1832, NC; 1780, Brentwood only.
Chelmsford: 2) 1781-1832, NC.
3) 1926-48, MY, MP.
Clavering: 2) 1780-1832, NC.
3) *(Walden division)* 1907-49, MY, MP.*
Dengie: 1) Maldon, 1710-18, SY [D/B 3/3/564].
2) 1781-1832, NC.
3) 1833-77, MY, MP.*
Dunmow: 2) 1780-1832, NC.
Freshwell:
1) 1762, 1766, 1775, 1777-79, MP [D/Z 2/7].
2) 1780-1832, NC.
3) pre-1865, SY, SP; 1936-49, MY, MP.
Harlow: 2) 1780-1832, NC.
3) *(Epping division)* 1921-49, MY, MP.*
Havering: 1) 1698, Complete [D/DMs 027/1-28].
2) 1794-1832, NC.
3) 1826-1924, MY, MP.

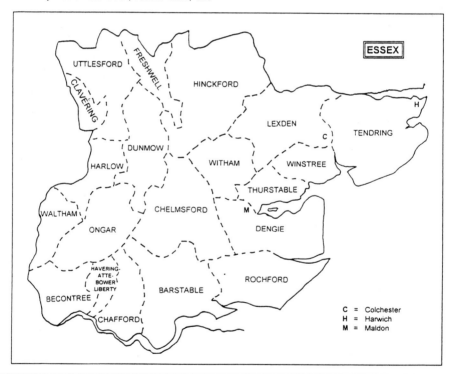

LTA = Land Tax Assessment; M = Many; NC = Near Complete; P = Parishes; S = Some; Y = Years

Essex continued

Hinckford:
1) 1726, 1766, 1775, 1777-9, MP [D/Z 2/7].
2) 1780-86, 1789-1832, NC.
3) 1833-1949, MY, MP.
Lexden: 2) 1781-1832; 1780, parishes in Witham division only.
3) pre-1922, MY, MP.
Ongar: 2) 1780-1832, NC.
3) 1936-45, MY, SP.
Rochford: 2) 1780-1832, NC.
Tendring: 1) Great Bromley, 1742 [D/DU40/49]; Great Clacton, 1743 [D/DRT108]; Harwich (St. Nicholas), 1775 [D/DU 457/14/1].
2) 1781-1831, NC; Harwich, 1786-1832.
Thurstable: 2) 1780-1832, NC.
Uttlesford:
1) Debden, 1773-7 [D/DFc 178, pp.144-8, 153-6].
2) 1780-1832, NC.
3) (Walden division) 1907-49, MY, MP.*
Waltham:
1) Sewardstone, 1738, 1740-2 [D/DHt 021].
2) 1780-1832, NC.
Winstree: 2) 1781-3, 1785-1832, NC.
3) pre-1922, MY, MP.
Witham: 2) 1780-1832, NC.
3) 1856-63, MY, MP.
Colchester Borough: 1) 1778 [Q/RP1].
2) 1781-1831, NC.
3) 1885, and post-1918, MY.

LB of Waltham Forest, Vestry House Museum, Vestry Road, London E17 9NH:

Walthamstow: 1) 1740-41.
2) 1785-1825, MY.
Leyton: 2) 1783-1825, MY (transcripts of originals now (probably) in **Essex R.O.**).

Public Record Office, Kew:
Whole County, 1798 [IR.23/27-29] (see page 9).

Window Tax

Essex Record Office, Chelmsford:

Dagenham, 1785 [D/Z 34].
Harwich, St. Nicholas, 1775 [D/DU 457/14/1,2].
Great Leighs, 1778 [D/P 137/28/2].
Maldon borough, n.d. [D/B 3/3/4/2].
Purleigh, 1824 [D/P 197/28/5].
Roxwell, 1760 [D/P 288/18/1].
Little Sampford, 1766 [D/DWm T64/17].
Witham, 1742 [D/Z 3].
Woodham Walter, 1752-62 [D/P 101/28/3].

Essex Record Office (Colchester and N.E. Essex), Colchester:

Great Tey, 1772-74, 1778 [D/P 37/28/2-3].
Wivenhoe, 1757-65, 1767 [D/P 277/28/2-3].

GLOUCESTERSHIRE and BRISTOL

Land Tax

Gloucestershire Record Office, Gloucester:

The main deposit of LTAs (1775-1832) for the County and City of Gloucester belongs to the Quarter Sessions archives [Q/Rel] and is arranged by year within each hundred. LTAs for the City of Gloucester are held separately. Isolated LTAs occur in a variety of collections.

LTAs for Bristol are held at the **Bristol Record Office** and at **Somerset Record Office**, see p. 30.

Gloucestershire

1) **Pre-1775** (isolated LTAs):
Chedworth, 1713, 1723, 1731, 1741-2, 1745-6, 1753, 1755-9, 1762, 1764, 1767; Harescombe, 1762, 1773; Stone, 1763; Bibury, 1768, 1774; Mangotsfield, 1768; Greet, 1771; Berkeley (upper), 1773; Withington, 1774; Shipton Moyne, 1700 [D1571/E304]; Stinchcombe, 1710, 1722 [P312 MI/4]; Tidenham, 1714 [D2700/14203]; Woolaston, [C2700/14209].

1 & 2) **1775-1832**: Each division complete or near complete, bundled by hundreds. For 1775 LTAs are missing for the hundreds of Barton Regis, Bledislowe, Kiftsgate-upper, Longtree and Rapsgate. Chipping Campden is included with Kiftsgate-lower. The 1775 LTAs have been repaired and are stored separately, but are part of the main series. Details of surviving returns 1776-1832 are available in the searchroom.

3) **Post-1832**: For C19, some LTAs for Brightwells Barrow, Berkeley-upper and Slaughter Hundreds, and some isolated LTAs in Whitstone and Cleeve Hundreds. For C20, some LTAs for Brightwells Barrow, Cheltenham, Dudstone and Kings Barton, Slaughter and Tewkesbury, and some isolated LTAs in Thornbury and Westminster-upper Hundreds.

City of Gloucester

2) 1798-1825: some LTAs; all parishes represented except possibly St. Aldgate's; frequency varies.
3) 1846-53, NC [D177, box 57]; 1854-1925 [D177, boxes 58-67]; LTAs interspersed with those of Dudstone and King's Barton, uncatalogued.

Cirencester Borough
[treated as a separate hundred in Q/Rel]

1 & 2) 1775-1832 NC.

Tewkesbury Borough
[incl. with Tewkesbury Hundred in Q/Rel]

1 & 2) 1775-84, 1786-9, 1791, 1808, 1810.
3) see under Gloucestershire.

LTA = Land Tax Assessment; M = Many; NC = Near Complete; P = Parishes; S = Some; Y = Years

Gloucestershire continued

Shakespeare Birthplace Trust Record Office,
Stratford upon Avon:

1) Adlestrop, 1768 [DM 18/8/4/20];
   Mickleton, 1701 [ER 13/12/3];
   Quinton, 1709-10 [ER 13/16/113].
2) Little Compton, 1797 [ER 13/8/1].

Public Record Office, Kew:
Gloucestershire (whole county), 1798
[IR.23/30,31] (see page 9).

City and County of Bristol

Bristol Record Office, Bristol:

1) **Pre-1780:** 1694-99, SP, SY; 1700-79, All P, SY.
2) **1780-1832:** 1780-1825, All P, MY; 1826-32, SP, SY.
3) **Post-1832:** 1833-49, All P, SY.

Somerset Record Office, Taunton:
City of Bristol: 1) 1766-7, SP.
 2) 1780-1832, SY, SP.

Public Record Office, Kew:
City of Bristol, 1798 (included with Somerset)
[IR.23/73].

Window Tax

Gloucestershire Record Office, Gloucester:

Alveston, 1782-85 [D2957/13(62-66)].
Fairford, 1804 [D333/X3].
Painswick, 1723 [Q/S04, Easter 1723].
Little Sodbury, 1762 [D871/X2].
Stinchcombe, 1710 [P312 M1/4].
Arlington, Barnsley, Bibury, Coln St. Aldwyn,
   Eastleach Martin, Eastleach Turville, Hatherop,
   Kempsford, Lechlade and Southrop,
   1804 [D1070/VII/62] (250 names).

Bristol Record Office:
Bristol (City), 1702-1808. All parishes, many years.
Wick and Abson (parish), 1764, 1776-78, 1781,
   1785-86 [P/Abs/T/1 (c-j)].

GLOUCESTERSHIRE and BRISTOL

B	= Berkeley (detached)
G	= Gloucester
DofL	= Duchy of Lancaster
LB	= Lower Berkeley
MD	= Middle Dudstone and King's Barton
UL&S	= Upper Langley and Swinehead
UpTew	= Upper Tewkesbury
UpTh	= Upper Thornbury
W	= Westminster

LTA = Land Tax Assessment; M = Many; NC = Near Complete; P = Parishes; S = Some; Y = Years

HAMPSHIRE

Land Tax

Hampshire Record Office, Winchester:

1) **Pre-1780:** *New Forest West*, 1774-5;
Winchester, 1705-79;
Alton North, Portsdown, 1692-1729;
Isolated LTAs; see under subject index;
See also **Southampton Archives Service** and
Southampton University.
2) **1780-1832** (1799-1832 on mf): *County*, good
coverage from 1800 (1802 usually missing);
arranged by place.
Winchester, 1782-99, 1805-6 only.
3) **Post-1832:** sporadic survivals, sometimes
amongst LTAs of different divisions from the
pre-1833 ones.

Divisions
Alton North: 1) Binsted, 1692, 1698, 1701, 1704,
1710, 1716, 1718, 1720 [3M51/539-46].
2) 1800, 1803-32, NC.
3) 1911-49, MY, MP.
Alton South: 2) 1798, SP; 1800, 1803-32, NC.
East Meon, 1795.
3) 1833-1900, MY, MP.
Andover: 1) See **Southampton University Library.**
2) 1800, 1803-32, NC; Amport, 1802.
3) 1833-1949, MY, MP.
Basingstoke: 2) 1800, 1803-32, NC.
Monk Sherborne, 1801.
3) 1911-49, MY, MP.

Fareham: 3) 1941-49, MP.
Fawley: 2) 1799-1800, 1803-32, NC.
3) 1936-49, MP; Upham, 1921.
Kingsclere: 2) 1800-1, 1803-32, NC.
3) 1922, 1924-28, SP; Laverstoke, Overton, 1923.
New Forest East: 2) 1799, 1803-32, NC; 1800, SP;
Dibden Liberty, 1801.
New Forest West: 1) 1775, Complete [24M64 and
31M91];
Avon and Ripley, Burton, 1774 [24M64].
2) 1797-1832, MY, MP;
Muccleshell and Muscliffe, 1796.
Portsdown:
1) Boarhunt, 1703-4, 1715-16 [5M50/1254-61];
Portchester, 1707 [5M50/1420];
Southwick, 1710, 1712, 1715, 1723-27, 1729
[5M50/1848-56];
Wymering with Hilsea, 1704-5, 1712
[5M50/1949-52].
2) 1800, 1803-32, NC; Fareham 1789; Durley
1799.
Romsey: 3) 1845-1944, MY, MP.
Southampton: see **Southampton A.S.**
Isle of Wight: 2) 1800, 1803-31, NC;
Whippingham, Yarmouth 1799; Niton, 1801.
Winchester: 1) 1703-79 [W/E9/4-6; these include
references to Window Tax].
2) 1780-99, 1804-5.
3) Winchester (St. Bartholomew Hyde, St. Law-
rence, St. Mary Kalendar, St. Maurice, St. Peter
Colebrook, St. Swithun, St. Thomas), 1903-4;
All parishes, 1913-23, 1927-29, 1936-49.

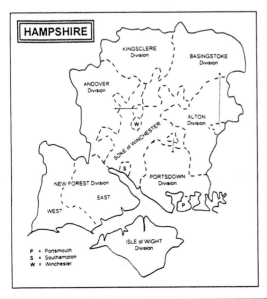

	Hundreds and Liberties	
	constituting Divisions	

Alton: Alton, Finchdean, East Meon, Selborne,
Bishop's Sutton.
Andover: Andover, Barton Stacey, King's
Somborne, Thorngate, Wherwell.
Basingstoke: Basingstoke, Bentley Lib.,
Bermondspit, Crondall, Holdshot,
Micheldever, Odiham.
Kingsclere: Chuteley, Evingar, Kingsclere,
Overton, Pastrow.
New Forest: Beaulieu Lib., Breamore Lib.,
Christchurch, Dibden Lib., Fordingbridge, New
Forest, Redbridge, Ringwood, Westover Lib.
Portsdown: Alverstoke Lib., Bosmere,
Fareham, Hambledon, Havant Lib.,
Meonstoke, Portsdown, Portsmouth and
Portsea Island Lib., Titchfield, Bishop's
Waltham.
Southampton town.
Isle of Wight: East and West Medina.
City of Winchester.
Soke of Winchester: Bountisborough,
Buddlesgate, Fawley, Mainsborough,
Mainsbridge.

LTA = Land Tax Assessment; M = Many; NC = Near Complete; P = Parishes; S = Some; Y = Years

Hampshire *continued*

Southampton Archives Services:
Southampton city: 1) 1711-78, MY, MP
[SC 14/2 118-386].
2) 1781-98, NC.

Southampton University Library
[Broadlands archive, formerly H.R.O. 27M60].
Andover: 1) Andover Extra, 1708, 1710;
Kings Somborne, 1708, 1715;
Thorngate Hundred, 1710;
Woodbury, 1711, 1716

Public Record Office, Kew:
Whole County, 1798 [IR.23/77,78] (see page 9).

Pinhorns, Normans, Newbridge, Yarmouth, Isle of
Wight PO41 0TY.
Index to Isle of Wight, 1798.

Window Tax

Hampshire Record Office, Winchester.
Winchester LT records [W/E9] include. refs. to WT.

Southampton Archives Services:
Southampton (City), 1732 (par. Holy Rood only);
1760-81, SY, MP.

Southampton University Library
Headbourne Worthy, 1714 [f'ly H.R.O. 27M60/L11].

Isle of Wight Record Office, Newport:
Newport (Borough), 1733 [45/264].

HEREFORDSHIRE

Land Tax

Hereford Record Office.

1) **Pre-1780:** sporadic survival, late 1770s; and
Greytree from 1747.
2) **1780-1832:** good coverage.
3) **Post-1832:** some survivals, 1833-38.

LTAs are in Q/REL/1-12, arranged by parish
within each hundred.

Hundreds
Broxash: 1) 1777-79, SY.
2) 1780-1831, All P, SY.
Ewyas: 2) 1781-1832, All P, SY.
3) 1833-38, All P, SY.
Greytree: 1) 1747-79, MP, SY.
2) 1780-1830, All P, SY.
Grimsworth: 1) Norton Canon, 1777-9
2) 1780-1830, All P, SY.
Huntingdon: 2) 1783-1832, All P, SY.
3) Winforton, 1833-6 SY.

Herefordshire *continued*

Radlow: 2) 1782-1830, All P, SY.
Stretford: 1) Pembridge, 1776-79 SY.
2) 1780-1830, All P, SY.
Webtree: 1) 1777-79, All P, SY.
2) 1780-1832, All P, SY.
3) 1833-8, MP, SY.
Wigmore: 2) 1782-1830, All P, SY.
Wolphey: 2) 1783-1830, All P, SY.
Wormelow: 1) 1774-9, All P, SY.
2) 1780-1831, All P, SY.
Hereford City: 2) 1794-1830, SY.
Leominster: 2) 1783-1831, SY.

National Library of Wales, Aberystwyth:
Much Dewchurch, 1798, 1803 [Mynde Park Deeds
and Documents, 2723, 2694].

Public Record Office, Kew:
Whole County, 1798 [IR.23/32] (see page 9).

Window Tax

Hereford Record Office:

Greytree Hundred (complete): 1776 [Q/RTw/1-18];

Parishes: Newton Llanveynoe, 1781 [Q/RTw/20-21].
Tarrington, 1697 [E12/F/Port 11; permission needed].
Tretire and Michaelchurch, 1787 [Q/RTw/23].
Upton Bishop, 1777 [Q/RTw/19].
Winforton and Willersey, 1783 [Q/RTw/22].

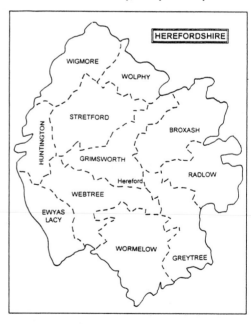

LTA = Land Tax Assessment; M = Many; NC = Near Complete; P = Parishes; S = Some; Y = Years

HERTFORDSHIRE

Land Tax

Hertfordshire Archives & Local Studies, Hertford:

1) **Pre-1780:** 1690, *Cashio, Dacorum* [D/EX294/Z1]; 1711-1767, *Cashio, Hertford, Braughing, Broadwater* (1753 almost complete).
2) **1780-1832:** good coverage (many gaps 1811-15); LTAs to 1832 arranged by parish.
All above (except 1690) now available on microfilm.
3) **Post-1832:** The Longmore deposit includes LTAs 1857-1891, 1936-1949.

Hundreds
St. Albans Borough: 1) 1753.
2) 1786-1825, MY.
3) 1896-1946, MY.
Cashio: 1) 1690, MP; 1713-80, SY, MP.
2) 1786-1829, MY, MP.
3) 1863-1946, SP, MY.
Hertford: 1) 1711-67, MY, MP.
2) 1780-1831, MY, MP.
3) 1863-5, 1889-91, 1911-46, NC.
Hitchin: 1) 1752-3, MP.
2) 1780-1830, MY, MP.
3) 1935-49, MY, MP.
Dacorum: 1) 1690, MP; 1746-53, MP, SY.
2) 1780-1805, MY, MP; 1825-31, SY, MP.
3) 1898-1946, MY, MP.
Braughing: 1) 1712-80, SY, MP.
2) 1780-1831, MY, MP.
3) 1916-39, MY, MP.
Broadwater: 1) 1715-57, MY, MP.
2) 1780-1811, 1825-31, MY, MP.
3) 1898-1946, MY, MP.
Odsey: 1) 1746-54, SY, MP.
2) 1780-1832, MY, MP.
3) 1832-6, 1936-49, MY, MP.
Edwintree: 1) 1746-53, MY, MP.
2) 1780-1832, MY, MP.
3) 1833-6, MY, MP.

Public Record Office, *Kew:*
Whole *County*, 1798 [IR.23/33] (see page 9).

Window Tax

Hertfordshire Archives & Local Studies, Hertford:

Broadwater Hundred, 1715-35 [LT.Misc.10], SY, MP.

Parishes: Little Munden, 1764 [LT.Misc. 10].
Braughing, 1746 [LT.Misc. 10].
Broxbourne, 1712-13 [LT.Misc. 10].
Bygrave, 1783 [LT Misc. 10].
Essendon, 1711-26 [D/P 37 8A/1].
Hoddesdon, 1785 [D/P 24A 29/1].
Kensworth, 1781 [LT.Misc. 10].
Totteridge, 1767-68 [68945].
Welwyn, 1723-40, 1763-75 [D/P 119 8/2,4].

Male Servants Tax, 1780

Published: Index to taxpayers, in *Middlesex and Hertfordshire Notes and Queries.* Index to whole country at **Society of Genealogists** (see page 14).

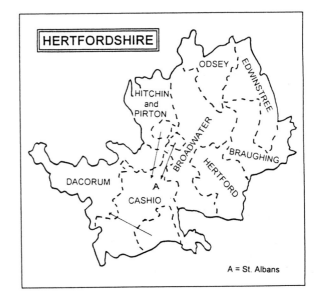

A = St. Albans

LTA = Land Tax Assessment; M = Many; NC = Near Complete; P = Parishes; S = Some; Y = Years

HUNTINGDONSHIRE

Land Tax

County Record Office, Huntingdon:

1) **Pre-1780:** 1767, most of *County* (indexed).
2) **1780-1832:** 1805-6, complete; most of *County* (except *Toseland*) then complete to 1832; *Toseland* from 1816 to 1832.
3) **Post-1832:** a few C20 LTAs for *Norman Cross* only.

LTAs are arranged by year; *Genealogical Sources in Cambridgeshire Record Office, Cambs. R.O., 1979,* gives years of surviving LTAs for each parish.

Hundreds
Huntingdon (Borough): 2) 1805-6.
Hurstingstone: 1) 1767, complete except for St. Ives.
  2) 1804-32, complete.
Leightonstone: 1) 1767, complete.
  2) 1805-32, complete.
Norman Cross: 1) 1767, NC.
  2) 1805 or 1806 to 1832, NC.
  3) a few C20 LTAs.
Toseland: 1) 1767, complete;
  1705-10, Hemingford Abbots only.
  2) 1805-6 (or 1805); 1816-32, complete.

Norris Museum and Library, St. Ives:
  St. Ives (Borough): 1) 1728.

Public Record Office, Kew:
  Whole *County*, 1798 [IR.23/34] (see page 9). Microfilm at *County Record Office, Huntingdon,* plus *Huntingdon* 1799; and 25 parishes 1800; see *Jnl Cambs FHS* **4** (5), Feb 1984.

Window Tax

County Record Office, Huntingdon:

Great Catworth, 1702 [DDM 5C/8].
Hemingford Abbots, 1709 [2537/9].
Kings Ripton, 1765-67 [2859/M/85-88].
Stanground, 1698, 1744-45, 1752 [2776/18/9-12].

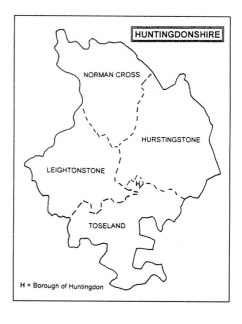

H = Borough of Huntingdon

KENT

Land Tax

Centre for Kentish Studies, Maidstone:

Pre-1780: St. Augustine East and West, good
survival; some also for Sutton at Hone Lower
(Bromley and Greenwich);
occasional years for other divisions [Q/CTI].
2) **1780-1832:** good survival [Q/RPI].
3) **Post-1832:** extensive C19 and C20 (mainly
1930-49) survivals [TC/La].

See under 'Land Tax' in index to the Guide to the
Kent County Archives Office and 1st and 2nd
Supplements.
The administration of the Land Tax in Kent was
more complex than that of its neighbouring
counties. The county administration was
responsible for raising 91 per cent of the Kentish
quota but the Cinque Port liberties and Canterbury
operated separate administrations. Records for
many of these have not survived. The county
administration was divided into divisions which tend
to follow the traditional subdivisions of the lathes.
The Land Tax assessment areas, called 'boroughs'
in certain parts of the county, notably Shepway
Upper and Lower, Scray Lower and the Tonbridge
division of Aylesford South, sometimes bear little
relationship to the ecclesiastical parishes.

Places with separate administrations:
Tenterden, Lydd, New Romney, Folkestone Town,
Hythe Liberty, Canterbury City, Dover Liberty,
Thanet Division, Fordwich, Sandwich Liberty,
Faversham Town.

Divisions
St. Augustine East (Wingham):
1) 1698-9, 1704-79, MY, MP.
2) 1780-1832, NC.
3) 1931-49, MY, MP.
St. Augustine West (Home): 1) 1723-79, MY, MP.
2) 1780-1832, NC.
3) 1943-9, MY, MP.
Scray Lower (Cranbrook): 1) 1756, 1759, MP.
2) 1780-1832, NC.
3) 1833-99, 1942-9, MY, MP.
Scray Upper (Milton and Teynham):
2) 1780-1832, NC.
Scray Upper (Faversham and Boughton):
2) 1780-1832, NC.
3) 1856,1871-3, 1880-1949, MY, MP.
Shepway Lower: 1) 1746, MP.
2) 1780-1832, NC.
Shepway Upper (Elham):
1) 1753, Folkestone parish only.
2) 1780-1832, NC.
Aylesford East (Bearsted): 1) 1744, 1746, 1753,
1755, 1760, 1768, 1774, 1779, MP.
2) 1780-1832, NC.

Aylesford South:
Malling: 1) 1754, 1764, 1769, Burham only.
2) 1780-1832, NC.
3) 1834-8, 1840, 1842-52, 1854-87, MY, MP.
Tonbridge: 2) 1780-1832, NC.
3) 1833-1938, 1942-9, MP, MY.
Aylesford North (Rochester): 2) 1780-1832, NC.
Sutton at Hone Lower (Sevenoaks):
2) 1780-1832, NC. 3) 1942-9, MY, MP.
Sutton at Hone Upper:
Bromley: 1) 1729-32, 1737-8, 1740-1, 1751-2,
1754-6, 1761-4, 1771, MP, SY.
2) 1780-1832, NC.
Greenwich: 1) 1707-9, 1725-40, 1747, 1753-65,
1772-5, SY, SP.
2) 1780-1832, NC.
3) 1857-1911, SY, SP.
Dartford: 2) 1780-1832, NC.

Originally separate administrations
New Romney Borough: 1689-1753, 1772-94, 1802-
1804, MY [NR/RTI].
Cinque Ports Liberty of Sandwich: Deal Borough,
1722, 1732, 1771 [De/RTI];
Sandwich Borough, 1718-93 [Sa/RTI].
Sandwich Division (Deal, Ramsgate, St. Nicholas at
Wade, Sandwich, Walmer), 1931-49 [TC/La].
Canterbury City: 3) 1943-9, MP, MY.
Cinque Ports Liberty of Dover: Acol and Birchington
1718-84; St John Thanet 1724-79; St Peter Thanet
1713-84 [U1453/01].
Dover Division: 3) Dover 1931-43, Ringwould 1931-
1949 [TC/La].
Thanet Division: 3) 1911-5, 1917-8, 1921-32, 1934-
1946, MP, MY [TC/La].
Fordwich: 3) 1943-9.
Faversham: 1) Borough 1739-62 [Fa/RTI];
2) Town and parish 1780-1832, MY [Q/RPI];
3) Town Division 1870-1949, MY [TC/La].

Records of individual parishes
Bredgar 1750-60 [U2140 02].
Cowden 1859 [U1612].
Hildenborough 1709 [U1866 04].
Keston 1768 [U1977 01].

Canterbury City and Cathedral Archives:
Canterbury City: 1 & 2) 1752-1797.

Lydd Borough Council(?):
Lydd Town: 2) 1798-1802, 1804-5.

Sevenoaks Library (Archives Dept.):
Sevenoaks and area (part of Sutton at Hone
Lower, 1702 (indexed) [U1000/20 O3].
Chevening, 1837-44, Seal 1815-44, Shoreham
1809 [U1000/20 O4-13].

Public Record Office, Kew:
Whole County, 1798 [IR.23/35-38] (see page 9).

LTA = Land Tax Assessment; M = Many; NC = Near Complete; P = Parishes; S = Some; Y = Years

Kent *continued*

Window Tax

Centre for Kentish Studies, Maidstone:

Divisions:
St. Augustine East (Wingham): 1705-88, MY, MP
[Q/CTi; Q.CTw and Q/CTz 1,2].
St. Augustine West (Home): 1722-85, MY, MP
[Q/CTi; Q/CTw and Q/CTz 1].
Aylesford East (Bearsted): 1774, 1778-79, 1783-86,
MP [Q/CTi and Q/CTw].
Scray Lower (Cranbrook): 1790, 1792-93 MP
[TC/W/Cr].

Separate administrations:
Canterbury City (see right).
Faversham 1739-58, 1785, NC [Fa/RTw 1-21].
Folkestone (see right).
New Romney 1696-1752, NC [NR/RTw 2-51].
Sandwich 1719-83, SY, MP
[Sa/RTh 1; Sa/RTw 1-14 and Sa/RTz 4].
Cinque Ports Liberty of Dover: Birchington, 1767-
1784, St. John Thanet 1747-85, St. Peter Thanet,
1748-85 (also some inhabited house tax and
servants' tax assessments) [U1453/02-04].

Parishes:
Farnborough, 1761-62; Knockholt, 1761-62, 1764;
Chislehurst and West Wickham, 1762
[U36/08,014, 018,020]
Keston, 1768 [U1977 01].
Meopham, 1711, 1720, 1735 [U1127/010/1-3].
Rodmersham, 1707-27 [P307/28/2].
Sarre, 1766 [U442/051].
Speldhurst, 1783-84 [U936/07].

Canterbury City and Cathedral Archives:
Canterbury (City), 1721-88, MY, MP
[B/C/O and B/C/W].
Walmer, par. St. Mary, 1766, 1768 [U3/60/18/7].

East Kent Archive Centre, Whitfield, Dover:
Folkestone, 1777-85 [FO/RT 1-15].

West Kent Branch Office, Sevenoaks Library:
Sevenoaks (Town and Weald) and Riverhead,
1712 [U1000/20 O2].

Bromley Central Library:
Ruxley Hundred and Bromley and Beckenham
Hundred (Sutton at Hone Lathe), 1765-67, 1771,
MP [T1-T16].

British Library (Manuscripts Collection):
Beckenham, and West Wickham, 1771
[Add.Mss. 42120A & C].

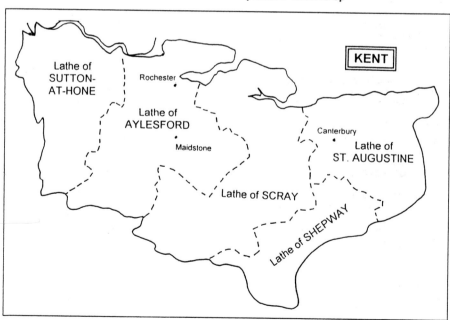

KENT

Lathe of SUTTON-AT-HONE
Rochester
Lathe of AYLESFORD
Maidstone
Canterbury
Lathe of ST. AUGUSTINE
Lathe of SCRAY
Lathe of SHEPWAY

LTA = Land Tax Assessment; M = Many; NC = Near Complete; P = Parishes; S = Some; Y = Years

LANCASHIRE

Land Tax

Lancashire Record Office, Preston:

1) **Pre-1780:** Clitheroe 1737, 1750.
   No other survivals.
2) **1780-1832:** varying coverage [QDL].
3) **Post-1832:** no survivals.

LTAs are arranged by year, and township within each hundred.

Divisions
Lonsdale (North and South): 1781-1831, NC.
Amounderness: 1781-1831, NC, except 1806 and 1816.
Blackburn: 1782-1831, NC, except 1799 and 1805.
Leyland: 1781-1831, NC.
West Derby: 1781-1831, NC.
Salford: 1780-1831, NC.
Audenshaw: SY, SP, 1824 only.
Liverpool: 1795, 1801, 1803-06, 1808-12, 1814-17, 1819-21, 1823-25, 1829-30. SP.
Manchester: 1784, 1786-7, 1791, 1794, 1796-1803, 1805-31, MP.
Preston: 1823-31.
Wigan: 1806-07, 1819, MP.

Cumbria Record Office, Barrow-in-Furness:

Ulverston, 1775-81, 1797 [St. Mary's parish collection].
Broughton-in-Furness, 1793.
Dalton-in-Furness, 1743-4.
Walney Island, 1798-1804.
Pennington, 1794 [BDY/167].

Manchester Local Studies Unit, Archives, Manchester Central Library.
Manchester 1798-1811, 1838 [M9/50/1-18].

Wigan Record Office, Leigh:

Abram, 1759 [D/DX Ta 19/16];
Atherton, 1755 [TR Ath F3].
Ince, 1724 [D/D An 68/11].
Lowton, 1693-1766 [D/P 17/24/1].

Public Record Office, Kew:
   Whole *County*, 1798 [IR.23/39-42] (see page 9).

Society of Genealogists:
   Woolstone, 1785, 1790, 1795, 1800, 1805, 1815.

Window Tax

Lancashire Record Office, Preston:

Altcar, n.d., *c.*1810 [PR 2474].
Ashton-under-Lyne, 1744 [PR 2577].
Bispham, 1799-1812 [PR 2596/17].
Burscough (tshp. in par. Ormskirk), 1773 [PR 1281].
Great Harwood (tshp. in par. Blackburn), 1762 [PR 162].

Manchester Central Library, Local Studies Unit:
Cheetham, 1823 [M10/7/8/1].

Wigan Record Office, Leigh:
Pennington, 1791 [Pennington Township Records].
Wigan, 1768 [Wigan Borough Records].

Warrington Library, Local History Collection.
Warrington, *c.*1792-98, 1803 [MS 187-197, 201-2, 208, 218].
Ashton-upon-Mersey, 1820-21, publ. *in Trans. Lancs. & Cheshire Antiq. Soc.* **61**, pp. 137-160.

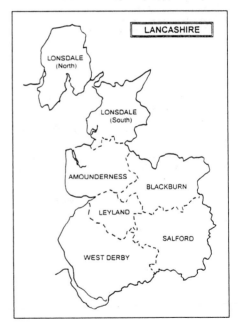

LEICESTERSHIRE

Land Tax

Leicestershire Record Office, Wigston Magna:

1) **Pre-1780:** 1773-4, complete for most of *County*, part for 1775-6 [QS/62/].
2) **1780-1832:** NC except for *Leicester* borough [QS/62/].
3) **Post-1832:** virtually no survivals.

LTAs are arranged by place and fully catalogued, with missing years noted.

Hundreds
East Goscote: 1) 1773, MP; 1774, NC.
  2) 1780-1832, NC (1791, MP only).
Framland: 1) 1773-6, NC.
  2) 1780-1832, NC.
Gartree: 1) 1773-5, NC.
  2) 1780-1832 (1813, SP only);
    Blaston, 1820; Denton, 1815 [3 D 40/17/3-10].
  3) Hallaton, 1850/7 [3 D 40/17/3-10].
Guthlaxton: 1) 1773-4, NC.
  2) 1780-1832, NC (1782 and 1797, MP only).
Leicester borough: 1) 1773-4.
  2) 1780; 1817-29.
Sparkenhoe: 1) 1773-4, NC.
  2) 1780-2, 1784-1830, NC.
West Goscote: 1) 1773-4, NC.
  2) 1780-1830, NC.
  3) 1919-47 - see under Derbyshire.

Public Record Office, Kew:
  Whole *County*, 1798 [IR.23/43, 44] (see page 9).

Window Tax

Derbyshire Record Office, Matlock:
  Netherseal, 1737 [D77M, box 23, folder 2].

Note. None found at **Leicestershire Record Office**.

LEICESTERSHIRE

FRAMLAND

WEST GOSCOTE

EAST GOSCOTE

SPARKENHOE

GARTREE

GUTHLAXTON

L = Borough of Leicester

LTA = Land Tax Assessment; M = Many; NC = Near Complete; P = Parishes; S = Some; Y = Years

LINCOLNSHIRE

Land Tax

Lincolnshire Archives, Lincoln:

For administrative purposes, including the Land Tax, Lincolnshire was divided into the three Parts of *Holland, Kesteven* and *Lindsey* plus the *City and County of Lincoln.* All four LTA collections are housed at the Archives Office.

HOLLAND

1) **Pre-1780:** significant survivals, earliest year 1724, Spalding 1743.
2) **1780-1832:** complete for some parishes, others terminating at 1811 or 1824.
3) **Post-1832:** a few from 1855 on.

LTAs are arranged by year.

Wapentakes:
Elloe including Spalding:
1) 1777-9 [Holland Deposit].
2) 1780-1811 [Holland Deposit];
1798 [LAO/KEST/IX];
1798-1824 [duplicate set, Holland Deposit].
Spalding only:
1) 1743 [Holland Deposit duplicates].
2) 1780-95 [Holland Deposit duplicates].
Kirton: 2) 1798 [LAO/KEST/IX].
Skirbeck: 1) 1777-9 [Holland Deposit].
2) 1780-1811 [Holland Deposit];
1798 [LAO/KEST/IX] Includes *Boston Borough* at least in LAO/KEST/IX.
North Holland (approx. equal to *Kirton* and *Skirbeck Wapentakes.* Might be Deanery area):
1) 1724-79, SY, SP [Holland Deposit].
2) 1780-1832, NC [Holland Deposit].
3) 1855, 1857-8, NC [Holland Deposit].

KESTEVEN

1) **Pre-1780:** no survivals.
2) **1780-1832:** 1798, 1808, 1812, 1817-9, 1824-5, 1827-32, Complete;
a few other years for some parishes.
Arranged by year.
3) **Post-1832:** considerable survivals, particularly *Aveland.*

Wapentakes (LT deposit unless otherwise stated; for pre-1833 see above):
Aswardhum: 1942-9, SY, all parts.
Aveland: 1832-49, SY, SP;
also 1838-61, SY, SP [LAO 2 TAX 4/10].
Beltisloe: 1942-9, SY, all P;
also Corby and Irnham, 1833-35 [Kest/IX].
Boothby Graffoe: 1910-49 SY, NC.
Flaxwell: 1942-49, SY, all P.
Grantham Soke and Borough: 1936-49, SY, all P.
Langoe: 1910-49, SY, NC.

Loveden: 1942-9, SY, all P.
Ness Wapentake and Stamford Borough:
1896-1929, SY, SP.
Winnibriggs: 1936-49, SY, all P.
Index to all Kesteven wapentakes, 1808.
Searches £2 p/surname: Wendy Atkin, 15 Castle Street, Sleaford, Lincs. NG34 7QE.

LINDSEY

1) **Pre-1780:** *Candleshoe,* 1695-1747, SY, MP; and a few for *Bolingbroke,* 1759-79.
2) **1780-1832:** considerable survivals, with main breaks in early 1780s.
Arranged by year [Lindsey Deposit].
3) **Post-1832:** variable survivals [Land Tax Deposit].

Wapentakes/Sokes:
Aslacoe: 2) 1782-1831, NC.
3) 1875-1949, SY, SP.
Bolingbroke: 1) 1759-60, 1764-5, 1767-9, 1722-4, 1776-9.
2) 1780-6, 1790-1832, NC.
3) 1831-1949, MY, MP.
Bradley Haverstoe:
2) 1782-3, 1786, 1789-1832, NC (but none for Grimsby borough).
3) 1923-46, SY, SP.
Calceworth: 2) 1780, 1782-6, 1791-1832, NC.
3) 1905-49, SY, SP.
Candleshoe: 1) 1695-1747, MP, SY [Lindsey Deposit 35/2).
2) 1780, 1782-3, 1785, 1790-1832, NC.
3) 1831-1949, MY, MP.
Corringham: 2) 1781-4, 1787-1831, NC.
3) 1925-49, SY, SP.
Gartree: 2) 1782-4, 1786, 1790-1832, NC.
3) 1899-1949, MY, SP.
Hill: 2) 1782-3, 1786-7, 1790-1832, NC.
3) 1841-7, Ashby Puerorum only.
Horncastle Soke: 2) 1781-3, 1790-1832, NC.
3) 1900-1949, MY, SP.
N.B. Horncastle parish, valuation to equalise the LT taken in 1813, in a private deposit [LAO/CHAT/5/16].
Lawress: 2) 1782-4, 1786, 1790-1828, NC.
3) 1875-1915, SY, SP.
Louth Eske: 2) 1781-6, 1790-1832, NC.
3) 1864-1949, SY, SP.
Ludborough: 2) 1780-5, 1790-1831, NC.
3) 1864-1949, SY, SP.
Manley: 2) 1782-4, 1786, 1790-1831, NC.
3) 1832-1949, MY, MP.
Walshcroft: 2) 1782-4, 1788, 1790-1832, NC.
3) 1885-1949, MY, MP.
Well: 2) 1782-4, 1786, 1790-1831, NC.
3) 1875-1915, SY, SP.
Wraggoe: 2) 1782-4, 1786, 1790-1832, NC.
3) 1875-1915, SY, SP.
Yarborough: 2) 1782-4, 1786, 1790-1831, NC.
2 & 3) 1805-42, in duplicate set, NC.

LTA = Land Tax Assessment; M = Many; NC = Near Complete; P = Parishes; S = Some; Y = Years

Lincolnshire continued

LINCOLN, County of the City

1 & 2) **Pre-1780; 1780-1832:** no survivals.
3) **Post-1832:** 1887-1949, MY (contents not checked).

Public Record Office, *Kew:*
Whole *County*, 1798 [IR.23/45-47] (see page 9).

See 'Early Land Tax Assessments Explored:
(1) Lincolnshire', by D.R.Mills, in *Land and Property:
The English Land Tax 1692-1832.*

Lincolnshire Archives, Lincoln:

Kesteven:
Dembleby, 1796-1812 [Dembleby Par.23].
Market Deeping, 1784 [Market Deeping Par.23/7].
Lindsey:
South Carlton, 1783, 1792-1800 and with Burton,
North Carlton and Broxholme, 1806-21 [South
Carlton Par.23/5/1,3-6].

LINCOLNSHIRE

MANLEY
YARBOROUGH
LINDSEY
BRADLEY
HAVERSTOE
CORRINGHAM
WALSHCROFT
LUDBOROUGH
ASLACOE
LOUTH ESKE
WELL
CALCEWORTH
LAWRES
WRAGGOE
GARTREE
HILL
CANDLESHOE
L
BOOTHBY
GRAFFOE
LANGOE
HORNCASTLE
BOLINGBROKE
FLAXWELL
KESTEVEN
LOVEDEN
B
SKIRBECK
ASWARDHURN
KIRTON
B = BOSTON
WINNIBRIGGS
& THREO
and
GRANTHAM
AVELAND
HOLLAND
BELTISLOE
ELLOE
NESS
L = City and Liberty
of LINCOLN

LTA = Land Tax Assessment; M = Many; NC = Near Complete; P = Parishes; S = Some; Y = Years

LONDON and MIDDLESEX

Land Tax

The bulk of LTAs are split between **London Metropolitan Archives** (formerly **G.L.R.O.**) and **Guildhall Library**; but there are also some at the **Tower Hamlets Central Library**.

Guildhall Library, Aldermanbury, London EC2P 2EJ:

The gigantic holdings (over 2,500 volumes) are listed briefly in *London Rate Assessments and Inhabitants Lists in Guildhall Library ...*, 2nd edition, 1968 (now out of print).

These consist of:
a) General assessments, covering the whole or a substantial part of the *City of London*, 1692-94, 1703-1949 (640 volumes), arranged by year.
b) LTAs for specific wards, some C18, mostly early C19.
c) LTAs for specific City parishes, for which the most extensive survivals are for St. Andrew Holborn, 1761-1826; St. Bride Fleet Street, 1708-1837; St. Giles Cripplegate, 1684-1810; and St. Sepulchre Holborn, 1758-1824 (most with substantial gaps). The latest are for 1837.
d) LTAs for parishes and liberties outside but close to the City:
Kensington division: Fulham, 1755-6; Paddington, 1730, 1733, 1746-8.
Tower division: many parishes from c.1730, through to 1832, and for ten parishes to c.1930.

London Metropolitan Archives
(formerly Greater London Record Office),
40 Northampton Road, London EC1R 0HB.

1) **Pre-1780:** 1693-4, for five *Middlesex* divisions [F34/1-289; facsimile copy of originals at the **Corporation of London Records Office**]; 1767, for whole *County of Middlesex* (except 24 parishes and liberties).
2) **1780-1832:** varying coverage for *Middlesex* (some duplicate holdings at **Guildhall** and **Tower Hamlets Libraries**).
3) **Post-1832:** few survivals, 1833, 1837-47.

LTAs are arranged by place.

Hundreds/Divisions (Middlesex)
Gore Hd.: 1) 1693-4, Complete.
2) 1780, 1782-1832, NC.
3) 1833, SP.
Kensington: 1) see **Guildhall Library**.
2) 1780, 1782-1832, NC.
Edmonton Hd.: 1) 1693-4, MP; 1767, NC.
2) 1780-1808, NC; 1809-29, MP, MY.
Isleworth Hd.: 1) 1693-94, MP;
2) 1780-1810, 1813-29, MY, MP.
Elthorne Hd.: 1) 1693-94, MP; 1767 NC.
2) 1780-1829, NC; 1830-33, MP.

Spelthorne Hd.: 1) 1693-94; 1767 NC.
2) 1780-1832, NC.
St. Giles (parish): 2) 1789-1832, NC.
Ossulstone Hd., Finsbury Div.: 1) 1767, NC.
2) 1780-1831, NC.
Ossulstone Hd., Holborn Div.: 2) 1789-1832, NC.
Ossulstone Hd., Tower Div.: 1) 1767, MP.
2) 1780-1832, NC (see also **Guildhall** and **Tower Hamlets Libraries**).
Westminster, St. Martin's in the Fields: 1) 1767, NC.
2) 1797-1832, M Wards, MY.
Westminster, St. George, Hanover Square:
2) 1781, 1797, 1801-31, M Wards, MY.
Westminster, St. Margaret: 1) 1767.
2) 1801-31, NC.
3) 1837-47, NC.
Westminster, St. Anne: 1) 1767.
2) 1801-31, MY, M Wards.
Westminster, St. James: 2) 1781, 1797-1832, M Wards, MY.
Westiminster, St. John: 1) 1767, NC.
2) 1801-31, NC.
3) 1837-40, 1846-47, NC.
Westminster: St. Paul, Covent Garden: 1) 1767, NC.
2) 1801-31, NC.

City of Westminster Archives Centre,
10 St. Ann's Street, London SW1P 2XR.

St. Anne Soho: 1 & 2) 1710-1829 (returns).
St. Margaret: 1-3) 1735-1845 (returns).
St. Marylebone: 2 & 3) 1801-85 (LTAs).

LB of Hackney Archives Department,
43 De Beauvoir Road, London N1 5SQ:

Shoreditch, St. Leonards:
1 & 2): 1744-1826, NC; 1926-36; also mf of 1806-1926 (origs. Guildhall Library).
Hackney: 1 & 2) 1727-1824, NC; also mf of 1827-1923 (gaps) (origs. Guildhall Library).
Stoke Newington: 2) 1821.

LB of Tower Hamlets Local History Library and Archives, *277 Bancroft Road, London E7 4DQ:*

1741-1826, St. Mary Bow, Bromley St. Leonard, St. Matthew Bethnal Green, Poplar and Blackwall (All SS Poplar), MY; St. Anne Limehouse, 1724; St. George-in-the-East, 1801 (published on m'fiche by East of London FHS, *Tower Hamlets, Miscellaneous Indexes*); Ratcliff, 1838; Liberty of the Old Artillery Ground, 1847.

LB of Waltham Forest, Vestry House Museum,
Vestry Road, London E17 9NH:
(covering area formerly in Essex)

Walthamstow: 1) 1740-1; 2) 1785-1825, MY.
Leyton: 2) 1783-1825, MY (transcripts of originals now (probably) in *Essex R.O.*

Buckinghamshire Record Office, Aylesbury.
Uxbridge 1949-50 [7/5].

LTA = Land Tax Assessment; M = Many; NC = Near Complete; P = Parishes; S = Some; Y = Years
---

London and Middlesex, Land Tax *continued*

Public Record Office, *Kew:*

London, 1798 [IR.23/56,57]; *Middlesex,* 1798 [IR.23/48/-52]; *St. George Hanover Square,* 1798 [IR.23/53]; *Westminster,* 1798 [IR.23/54,55] (see page 9).

| **Window Tax and other tax returns** |

City of London - none traced.

Middlesex

Central Reference Library, LB of Islington:
Window Tax: *Islington,* 1751-5, 1757, 1760, 1762, 1765-68, 1772, 1774-85.

City of Westminster Archives Centre.
St Anne Soho: Window tax, 1757;
Taxes on houses, windows, carriages, male servants, horses and dogs, 1796-97.
St. Margaret: taxes of windows, houses, carriages, horses, dogs and servants, 1747-1804.
St. Martin-in-the-Fields: taxes on shops, servants, horses, dogs, carriages and wagons, 1782-98.
St. Paul Covent Garden: window tax assessments, 1711-46.

Public Record Office, *Kew:*
Westminster, St. James Piccadilly, 1736 [T38/782] (3,600 names).

| **Male Servants Tax, 1780** |

Published: Index to taxpayers, in *Middlesex and Hertfordshire Notes and Queries.* Index to whole country at **Society of Genealogists** (see page 14).

| LTA = Land Tax Assessment; M = Many; NC = Near Complete; P = Parishes; S = Some; Y = Years |

MONMOUTHSHIRE

Land Tax

Gwent County Record Office, Cwmbran:

1) **Pre-1780:** Itton parish *(Caldecot Hundred)* only 1716, 1733, 1735 [D.Pa.3.36].
Bedwellty, Mynyddmaen hamlets, 1754 (mf).
2) **1780-1832:** whole *County* 1792-32, SY, MP.
Quarter Sessions records, arranged by constablery; for some places only a few LTAs for 1804-31.
Usk division: 1819-20, 1827, 1830 [LT Commissioners' deposit].
Note. In addition the G.R.O. holds many LTAs for individual places or areas, 1799-1827, which may or may not duplicate those in the Q.S. records. List available at G.R.O.
3) **Post-1832:** All parishes, 1868-1949 (LTAs and collector's duplicates). Also some LTAs for some individual places and years, which may or may not duplicate the above.

Divisions (post-1832 LTAs only):
Abergavenny: 1921-49.
Bedwellty: 1910-23.
Caerleon: 1868-80, 1904-49.
Chepstow: 1933-49.
Christchurch: 1898-1949.
Monmouth: 1921-49.
Newport: 1911-49 (see also **Glamorgan**, page 70).
Pontypool: 1867-1949.
Raglan: 1921-49.
Skenfrith: 1921-49.
Trellack: 1921-49.
Usk: 1921-49.

National Library of Wales, Aberystwyth:
[TPC = Tredegar Park Collection]

1 & 2) 1698-1731, 1743-1802, MY (Bassaleg, Bedwas, Bedwellty, Coedkernew, Henllys, Machen, Malpas, Marshfield, Michaelstow Vedow, Monythusloyne, Newport borough, Peterstone, Risca, Rumney, St, Brides, St. Mellans, St. Woolos). [TPC 68/43; 85 (4 boxes 1-724, 725-1264, 1265-1768, 1769- 2561, see schedule); 114; 768].
Llandeilo Gresynni 1685-1819 [Llangibby B757-9].
Monmouth town 1705 [M.P. Watkins/Vizard & Son].
Glasgoed 1776 [Llangibby B752].
Rockfield 1792 [L.T. Davies Colln., 46].
Llantrisent, Llansoy, Llandenny, Rockfield, 1799 [P.M. Hardwick's estate in, L.T. Davies Colln., 65].
Gwehelog, Llantrissent, Llan-gwm, Llanhenwg Fawr, 1821 [J. Conway Davies Papers, 19].
Betwys Newydd, Bryngwyn, Penyclawdd, Clytha, Digestow, Llanarth, Llandenny, Penrose, Raglan, Tregare, 1860-71 [L.T. Davies Colln. 8074-8111, 8120-8208].

Public Record Office, *Kew:*
Whole *County,* 1798 [IR.23/58] (see page 9).

Window Tax

National Library of Wales, *Aberystwyth:*

1706-9, Newport borough, parishes of St. Woollos, Bassaleg, St Bride's, Coedkernew, Bettwys, Malpas, Rumney, Henllis, Maughan, St Melons, Riska, Marshfield, Peterstone, Michallston y Vedw, Monythysloyne, Bedwellty and Bedwas [Tredegar Park Collection [TPC] 85/66-89, 2368-2409].
Wentllooge Hundred: 1752, 1779, 1794, MP [TPC 53/ 42-46; and 85/ 2416-2459].
Newport (Borough): 1728, 1746, 1750*, 1752, 1768 [TPC 20/3; 67/173, 85/2410, 2415, 2439].
Parishes/Places:
Marshfield and Bedwellty, 1746 [TPC 85/2411-14].
St. Mellons, Rumney and Henllys, 1768* [TPC 53/ 18, 20 and 21].
Marshfield, Coedkernew, St. Mellons, Peterstone and Michaelstone-Fedwy, 1779* [TPC 53/42-46].
Machen and Risca, 1780 [TPC 85/ 2440-41].
Rogerstone (Bassaleg), 1786-7 [TPC 97/247].
Monmouth (town), 1800 (incomplete) [L.T. Davies Collection, 8050].

Note. Items asterisked are also available at **Gwent Record Office,** *Cwmbran,* on Mf.239.

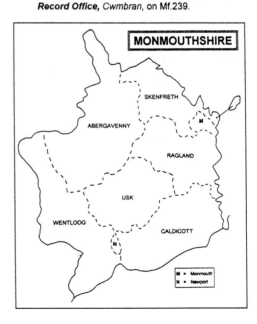

MONMOUTHSHIRE

SKENFRETH

ABERGAVENNY

RAGLAND

USK

WENTLOOG

CALDICOTT

M = Monmouth
N = Newport

NORFOLK

Land Tax

Norfolk Record Office, Norwich:

1) **Pre-1780:** 1767, 1777, several div'ns; 1695, *East and West Flegg* (transcribed by D.A. Tooke; copies at Norfolk Studies Library, Norwich, N&NGS; Soc. of Gen; Inst H&GS); 1702-14, *Happing, Tunstead.*
2) **1780-1832:** good coverage 1800-32; earlier years, varying coverage.
3) **Post-1832:** several deposits, unlisted and unsorted, thought to be very incomplete for C19, more C20 survivals.

All LTAs pre-1833 are arranged by place, with a typed guide. Norwich returns are listed in *Norwich City Records. Sectional Lists*, pp. 65a and 65b; and those for Great Yarmouth in *Guide to the Great Yarmouth Borough Records*, 1972, p. 53.

Divisions

Blofield: 2) 1781, 1789, All P; 1800-32, NC.
Clackclose: 1) 1767, All P.
  2) 1783-4, 1786, All P; 1789-1832, Complete.
Clavering: 2) 1798, MP; 1800-32, NC.
Depwade: 2) 1797, 1800-32, Complete.
Diss: 2) 1800-32, NC.
Earsham: 2) 1797, All P; 1799-1832, NC.
North Erpingham: 2) 1780, 1784, All P; 1786-1832, NC except 1790-1, 1799.
South Erpingham: 2) 1800-32, NC.

Eynsford: 2) 1801-32, NC.
East Flegg: 1) 1695 [Petre Cal., p.171].
  2) 1782, 1784, All P; 1786-32, Complete except 1789-92, 1794-6, 1812-4.
West Flegg: 1) 1695 [Petre Cal., p.171].
  2) 1782, 1784, 1786-9, NC; 1793-1832, Complete except 1794-5.
Forehoe: 1) 1767, NC.
  2) 1800-32, Complete except 1801.
Freebridge Lynn: 1) 1767, NC; 1777, All P.
  2) 1782, 1784, 1786-1832, NC.
Freebridge Marshland: 2) 1782, 1785-1832, NC, except 1787, 1791.
Gallow: 2) 1786-1832, NC, except 1791, 1793, 1798-9.
North Greenhoe: 2) 1782-1832, NC, except 1783, 1785-6, 1791 and 1798-9.
South Greenhoe: 1) 1778, All P.
  2) 1781-1832, NC, except 1783, 1790.
Grimshoe: 2) 1782-1832, NC, except 1783 and 1791.
Guiltcross: 1) 1767
  2) 1781-1797, MY, MP; 1800-32, Complete.
Happing: 1) 1702-14 [Petre Cal. pp.148-52].
  2) 1781, 1789, 1800-31, Complete.
Henstead: 2) 1782, 1785-8, 1792-97, 1800-32, NC.
Holt: 1) 1767, MP.
  2) 1786-9, 1796-1832, NC except 1798-9.
Humbleyard: 2) 1801-32, All P.
Launditch: 1) 1767, Stanfield only.
  2) 1782, 1791, 1800-32, NC.
Loddon: 2) 1798-1832, NC.

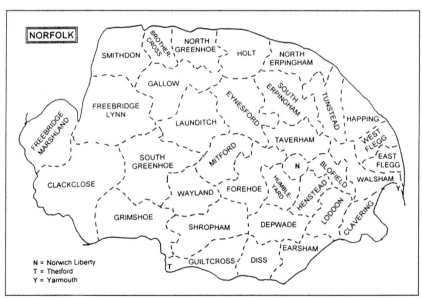

NORFOLK

SMITHDON
BROTHER-CROSS
NORTH GREENHOE
HOLT
NORTH ERPINGHAM
GALLOW
SOUTH ERPINGHAM
TUNSTEAD
FREEBRIDGE LYNN
EYNESFORD
HAPPING
FREEBRIDGE MARSHLAND
LAUNDITCH
TAVERHAM
WEST FLEGG
EAST FLEGG
SOUTH GREENHOE
MITFORD
N
HUMBLEYARD
BLOFIELD
WALSHAM
CLACKCLOSE
WAYLAND
FOREHOE
HENSTEAD
LODDON
CLAVERING
GRIMSHOE
SHROPHAM
DEPWADE
EARSHAM
N = Norwich Liberty
T = Thetford
Y = Yarmouth
GUILTCROSS
DISS

LTA = Land Tax Assessment; M = Many; NC = Near Complete; P = Parishes; S = Some; Y = Years

Mitford: 2) 1784-1832, NC, except 1788, 1790-2 and 1794-7.
Shropham: 1) 1767, All P.
2) 1781-4, 1796, 1798, 1800-32, NC.
Smithdon Brothercross: 1) 1777, NC.
2) 1783-1832, NC, except 1790-91.
Taverham: 2) 1789, 1800-32, All P.
Tunstead: 1) 1702-14 [Petre Cal. 148-52].
2) 1781-2, 1789, 1800-31, All P.
Walsham: 2) 1789, 1801-32, NC.
Wayland: 2) 1779-80, 1782, 1784-1832, NC, except 1791.
King's Lynn: 1) 1693-1705, SY [on microfiche].
Norwich: 1) 1710-79, SY, SP.
2) 1780-1832, SY, SP.
Great Yarmouth: 1) 1750, 1777, some wards.
2) No survivals.
3) 1936-49.

Public Record Office, *Kew:*

Whole *County*, 1798 [IR.23/59-61];
City of *Norwich*, 1798 [IR.23/62] (see page 9).

Window Tax

Norfolk Record Office, *Norwich:*

Norwich (city), 1708-65, SY, MP [Case 23/1-46].
Great Yarmouth (borough), 1768, 1771-72, 1781-82 [Y/D41].
Guestwick, 1732 [BUL 6/3 614x8].
East Harling, 1734 [PD219/172].
West Beckham, 1758; Erpingham, 1759; Cawston, c.1760, and Banningham, 1760 [BUL 4/21 605x8].

NORTHAMPTONSHIRE
(including the **Soke of Peterborough**)

Land Tax

Northamptonshire Record Office, *Northampton:*

1) **Pre-1780:** 1752-79, varying survivals.
2) **1780-1832:** Near complete for all Hundreds (1832 missing for Chipping Warden, Fawsley, Greens Norton, Kings Sutton and Polebrook only).
3) **Post-1832:** varying survivals, mostly C20.

LTAs are arranged by year, within each Hundred, with a catalogue to periods 1 and 2 (1746-1832) kept in the Catalogue Room [LT Record Book, X2295]. Post-1832 LTAs are also listed, refer to archivist.

For *Soke of Peterborough (Nassaburgh Hundred),* see page 46.

Hundreds (for 1780-1832 see above):
Chipping Warden:
3) 1896, 1901-22, 1935-1948, MY, MP.
Cleley: 1) 1774-5, 1778, NC [all in Grant (Litchborough) Collection].
3) 1903-49, MY, MP.
Corby: 1) 1752-5, 1774, NC.
3) 1847-1945, MY, MP.
Fawsley: 1) 1752-75, NC.
3) 1896-1949, MY, MP;
Daventry Town, 1833-85, MY.
Greens Norton: 3) 1903-49, MY, MP.
Guilsborough: 1) 1752-75, NC.
3) 1896-1949, MY, MP.
Hamfordshoe:
1) 1751, 1753-8, 1762-4. 1774-79, NC.
3) 1916-45, SY, SP.
Higham Ferrers:
1) 1751, 1753-8, 1762, 1764, 1774-79, NC.
3) 1916-45, SY, SP.
Huxloe: 1) 1752-5, 1774, NC.
3) 1847-1945, MY, MP.
Kings Sutton: 3) 1896, 1901-22, 1935-48, MY, MP.
Nassaburgh - **see page 46,** *Soke of Peterborough.*
Navisford: 1) 1775-9, NC.
3) 1912-35, MY, MP.
Nobottle Grove: 1) 1771-9, NC.
3) 1910-49, SY, SP.
Northampton Borough: 2) 1783 (West and Chequer Wards only).
Orlingbury: 1) 1753-8, 1762, 1764, 1774-9, NC.
3) 1910-49, SY, SP.
Polebrook: 1) 1775-9, NC.
3) 1912-35, MY, MP.
Rothwell: 1) 1752-5, 1774, NC.
3) 1847-1945, MY, MP.
Spelhoe: 1) 1772-9, NC.
3) 1910-49, SY, SP.

LTA = Land Tax Assessment; M = Many; NC = Near Complete; P = Parishes; S = Some; Y = Years

Northamptonshire continued

Towcester: 1) 1774-5, 1778, NC [all in Grant (Litchborough) Collection].
3) 1903-49, MY, MP.
Willibrook: 1) 1775-9, NC.
3) 1912-35, MY, MP.
Wymersley: 1) 1771-1832, NC.
3) 1910-49, SY, SP.

Soke of Peterborough

This now forms part of Cambridgeshire, and consequently its parishes appear in *Genealogical Sources in Cambridgeshire: A Summary List*, by Cambs. R.O., 2nd edition, 1994. This gives years of surviving LTAs for each parish.

Nassaburgh Hundred:
1) 1767, Lutton and Luddington only.
2) 1792-1832, MY, MP.
3) 1833-1948, MY, MP.

Public Record Office, *Kew:*
Whole *County,* (including *Soke of Peterborough*), 1798 [IR.23/63,64] (see page 9).

Window Tax

Northamptonshire Record Office, *Northampton:*

Hundreds: *Rothley, Corby and Huxloe,* 1702 [C(TM)92]; *Cleyley,* 1769, 1772, 1774-75, 1778; *Towcester,* 1768, 1772, 1774-75 and 1778 [both Grant of Litchborough X5273; X5317, A10]. *Higham Ferrers,* 1750 [X.2255].

Parishes: Brington, 1782 [SOX 6, item 1c]. Cransley, 1768, 1773, 1777 [89P/122-125]. Daventry, 1770-78 [96P/136 and 138-148]. Floore, 1775, 1784, 1786, 1790/1 [129P/206-209]. Harringworth, 1771 [156P/84]. Titchmarsh, 1785 [ZB 73/22]. Wellingborough, 1781-82, 1789 [YZ1263, YZ4642].

NASSABURGH or PETERBOROUGH Liberty

WILLYBROOK

CORBY · POLEBROOK

ROTHWELL

NAVISFORD

HUXLOE

GUILSBOROUGH · ORLINGBURY

HAMFORDSHOE

HIGHAM FERRERS

SPELHOE

NOBOTTLE GROVE · N

FAWSLEY

WYMERSLEY

CHIPPING WARDEN · GREENS NORTON · TOWCESTER

CLELEY

N = Northampton

KINGS SUTTON

NORTHAMPTONSHIRE

LTA = Land Tax Assessment; M = Many; NC = Near Complete; P = Parishes; S = Some; Y = Years

NORTHUMBERLAND

Land Tax

Northumberland Record Office, North Gosforth, Newcastle upon Tyne:

Microfilm copies of pre-1832 LTAs:
1) **Pre-1780:** 1748-53, complete *(County)* except 1751 for four divisions; 1760s and 1770s, isolated years; 1777-9, complete for *County*.
2) **1780-1832:** 1806-31, fair coverage; 1780-1, 1791, Tyndale only.

Morpeth Records Centre (Northumberland Record Office):

Originals of (1) and (2) above; also
3) **Post-1832:** 1848 Norham and Islandshire only. After 1863 division is by Union rather than Ward, for 1863, 1869, 1877 and 1885 only, incomplete. LTAs are arranged by year.

Division
Tynedale: 1) 1748-53, 1766, 1770-74, 1779, NC.
 2) 1780-1, 1791, 1805-6, 1811-4, 1817-8, 1822-31, NC.
Coquetdale: 1) 1748-53, 1765, 1767-9, 1771-4, 1777-9, NC.
 2) 1806-31, MY.
 3) 1863, NC.
Morpeth: 1) 1748-9, 1751-3, 1766, 1768-9, 1771-4, 1777-9, NC.
 2) 1806, 1809, 1811-31, NC.
 3) 1863, 1869, 1877, NC.
Bamburgh: 1) 1748-9, 1751-3, 1766, 1768-9, 1771-4, 1777-9, NC.
 2) 1806-31, MY.
Castle: 1) 1748-9, 1751-3, 1768-9, 1771-2, 1774, 1777-9, NC.
 2) 1806, 1809-31, NC.
 3) 1869, 1877, 1885, NC.
Glendale: 1) 1748-9, 1751-3, 1765, 1768, 1771-4, 1777-9, NC.
 2) 1806, 1809-12, 1817, 1823-31, NC.
 3) 1869, 1877, 1885, NC.
Newcastle: 1 & 2) None
 3) 1885, NC (see right).
Berwick: 1 & 2) None.
 3) 1869, 1877, 1885, NC.
Norham and Islandshire: 1 & 2) See Co. Durham, page 27.
 3) 1848, NC.

Other Unions:
Alnwick: 3) 1863, 1877, NC.
Bellingham: 3) 1869, 1877, 1885, NC.
Haltwhistle/Rothbury: 3) 1869, 1877, 1885, NC.

Tyne and Wear Archives Service, *Newcastle:*

Castle Ward, East Division:
Parishes: All Saints (incl. Byker and Heaton), 1833-1937.
Earsdon, 1833-1946.
Gosforth, 1833-1946.
Longbenton (incl. Walker and Weetslade), 1833-1937
Newburn, 1833-1936.
North Shields, 1833-1946.
St. John (incl. Benwell, Elswick, Fenham and Scotswood), 1833-1946.
Tynemouth, 1833-1946.
Wallsend, 1833-1913.
City Ward (Newcastle upon Tyne):
Parishes: All Saints 1737-1946;
St. Andrew 1769-1946;
St. John 1748-1946;
St. Nicholas 1748-1946.

Public Record Office, *Kew:*
Whole *County*, 1798 [IR.23/65,66] (see page 9).

For Bedlington(shire), see Co. Durham, page 27.

Window Tax

None traced.

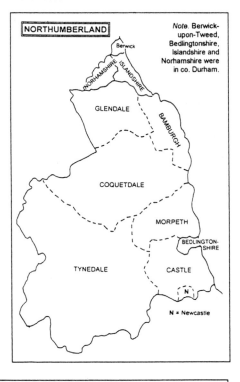

NORTHUMBERLAND

Note. Berwick-upon-Tweed, Bedlingtonshire, Islandshire and Norhamshire were in co. Durham.

Berwick

NORHAMSHIRE

ISLANDSHIRE

GLENDALE

BAMBURGH

COQUETDALE

MORPETH

BEDLINGTON-SHIRE

TYNEDALE

CASTLE

N

N = Newcastle

LTA = Land Tax Assessment; M = Many; NC = Near Complete; P = Parishes; S = Some; Y = Years

NOTTINGHAMSHIRE

Land Tax

Nottinghamshire Archives, Nottingham:

1) **Pre-1780:** 1700, *Newark Wapentake*; 1752-3, *Bassetlaw Wapentake*; 1753, 1758-9, *Nottingham borough.*
2) **1780-1832:** NC (except Thrumpton and Nottingham borough), 1781-1832 (1780 also for *Broxtowe South, Newark, Rushcliffe* and *Thurgarton North* and *South*).
3) **Post-1832:** *Newark* and *Thurgarton North* Wapentakes, extensive to 1927; *Thurgarton South*, 1830-58; otherwise random.

LTAs (pre-1833) are arranged by place.

Wapentakes (for 1780-1832 see above):
Bassetlaw, Hatfield and North Clay divisions:
 1) 1752-3, NC.
Bassetlaw, South Clay division:
 1) 1704, Bevercotes only *[Nottingham University MSS. Dept.]*; 1752-3, NC.
 3) 1840, Rampton; 1863-4, Laxton.
Bingham: 1) 1731, Car Colston [DD. SK 189/23]; 1761-80, Cropwell Butler.
 3) 1840-1927, Staunton; 1884-93, Cropwell Butler; 1882-8, Tollerton.
Broxtowe, North: 1) 1740, Kirkby in Ashfield only.
 2) 1780, 1800, Manfield. Indexes published by Mansfield & District FHS.
 3) 1854-66, Mansfield and Mansfield Woodhouse only.
Broxtowe, South: 1) 1737, Beeston only *[Nottingham University MSS. Dept.]*; 1750-80, Strelley only.
 3) 1857-65, Radford only.
Newark: 1) 1700, MP.
 3) 1838-1927, NC.
Newark Borough: 2) 1780-90, 1792-94, 1796-97, 1799-1803, 1806-08, 1811-16, 1818-22, 1824-32.
 3) 1875, only.
Nottingham Borough: 1) 1753, 1758-9 only.
 2) Nil.
 3) 1848-66 plus isolated examples.
Rushcliffe: 1) West Bridgford, 1697-1707, 1763 [DD.PF 123/107-8], 1770-80.
Thurgarton, North: 3) 1836-1927, NC.
Thurgarton, South 3) 1830-58, MY, MP.

Nottinghamshire Archives also has the original of a Subsidy of 1696 for a tax similar to the land tax (see page 4) which was published as *Nottinghamshire Subsidies, 1689*, ed. George Marshall, republished by Notts FHS, vol. **24**. This covers most of the county.

Sheffield Archives.
Worksop, 1728, 1762, 1774 [ACM W25].

Public Record Office, *Kew:*
Whole *County, 1798* [IR.23/67,68] (see page 9).

Window Tax

Nottinghamshire Archives, Nottingham:

Bilborough, 1781 [PR 1595].
Cuckney, 1758-1814 [PR 2726-2744].
Edwinstowe, 1778-1807 [PR 2131].
East Leake, 1811-12 [PR 21,978].
Strelley, 1764-77 [PR 1655].
Thorney, 1742 [DDN 213/2].

Income Tax

Nottinghamshire Archives, *Nottingham.*
Newark, 1806-7 (Schedule 'D' returns on profits of trade).

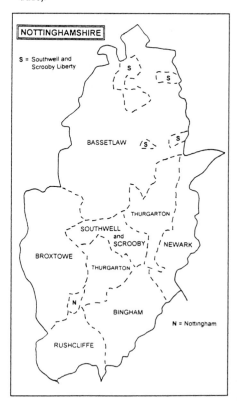

NOTTINGHAMSHIRE

S = Southwell and Scrooby Liberty

BASSETLAW

THURGARTON

SOUTHWELL and SCROOBY

NEWARK

BROXTOWE

THURGARTON

BINGHAM

N = Nottingham

RUSHCLIFFE

LTA = Land Tax Assessment; M = Many; NC = Near Complete; P = Parishes; S = Some; Y = Years

OXFORDSHIRE

Land Tax

Oxfordshire Archives, Oxford:

1) **Pre-1780:** 1705. Bodicote, Parish Accounts for
the 'Town' of Bodicote, 1700-1822, ed. J.H.
Fearon, Banbury Hist. Soc. 12, 1975. (pp.100-2).
1753, *Banbury Hundred* [private collection,
photocopy at *O.A.*]. Published and indexed in
Cake & Cockhorse **12**.4 (B.H.S., 1992).
2) **1780-1832:** 1785-1832, good coverage.
3) **Post-1832:** virtually no LTAs.

LTAs are arranged by places, and a list showing
what LTAs survive or are missing for each is
published in *The Oxfordshire Family Historian*, **3**, 1
(Spring, 1983).

Hundreds (all parishes, most with odd years
missing):
Bampton: 2) 1785-1831 (MP missing 1809; SP
missing 1790, 1798, 1800).
Banbury: 1) 1753, Complete, published (see
above).
　2) 1785-1831 (MP missing 1808).
Binfield: 2) 1785-1832 (MP missing 1812).
Bloxham: 2) 1785-1831 (All P missing 1794;
MP missing 1800, 1809; SP missing 1790,
1796).
　3) Drayton only, 1836.
Bullingdon: 2) 1785-1832 (SP missing 1794, 1796,
1809, 1811).
Chadlington: 2) 1785-1831 (SP missing 1798).
Dorchester: 2) 1785-1832 (All P missing 1809;
MP missing 1796; SP missing 1798, 1804).
Ewelme:
　2) 1785-1832 (MP missing 1786, 1806, 1811).
　3) Ewelme (parish) only, 1836.
Faringdon (Grafton and Radcot only):
　2) 1785-1831 (Grafton missing 1793).
Langtree: 1) Goring, 1774 [Misc.Bod.I/1].
　2) 1785-1832 (MP missing 1785, 1796, 1799,
1803-4, 1808, 1811).
Lewknor: 2) 1786-1832 (SP missing 1794, 1797,
1802, 1805).
Oxford city: 2) 1826 only.
Pirton: 2)1785-1832 (MP missing 1794 or 1795;
SP missing 1785, 1799, 1810).
Ploughley: 1) 1760, NC.
　2) 1786-1832 (All P missing 1793, 1815).
Thame: 2) 1785-1832 (MP missing 1787, 1808-9).
Wootton: 1) 1760, NC; 1762, SP;
　Northleigh only 1706-11, 1713-15, 1717-22
　2) 1785-1831 (MP missing 1785; SP missing 1795,
1800).

Public Record Office, *Kew:*
　Whole *County*, 1798 [IR.23/69] (see page 9).

Window Tax

Oxfordshire Archives, Oxford:

Deddington, 1748 [MSS.DD.Par.Deddington c32].
Lower Heyford, 1747 [MSS.DD.Par.L'r Heyford c4].
Over Norton, 1785-96 [Par.64/5/F3].
Warborough, 1783 [MSS.DD.Par.Warborough c8].

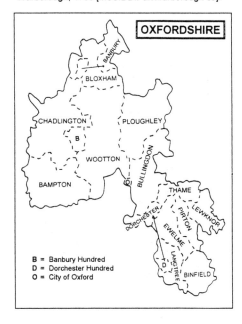

OXFORDSHIRE

BLOXHAM

CHADLINGTON　　PLOUGHLEY

B

WOOTTON

BULLINGDON

BAMPTON

THAME

LEWKNOR

DORCHESTER

PIRTON

EWELME

LANGTREE

BINFIELD

B = Banbury Hundred
D = Dorchester Hundred
O = City of Oxford

LTA = Land Tax Assessment; M = Many; NC = Near Complete; P = Parishes; S = Some; Y = Years

RUTLAND

Land Tax

Leicestershire Record Office, Wigston Magna:

1) **Pre-1780:** 1712 whole *County* [Finch Mss.
   DG7/4/1];
   1722 Empingham *(East Hundred)*, Normanton
   and Hambleton *(Martinsley Hundred)*
   [DG7/1/17/14,15];
   1760: Branston *(Oakham Hundred)*
   [DG7/1/17/13].
   See 'Early LTAs Explored: Rutland', by D.R.Mills,
   in *Land and Property*.
2) **1780-1832:** None (destroyed with other Quarter
   Sessions records).
3) **Post-1832:** 1862-3, 1865-1937, almost complete
   for whole *County* [DE 3256/10-12, 14-83].
   1836, 1838, 1841-1, 1843-4, 1856-7, 1864-5,
   Essendine only [DE 3256/5-9, 13].
   1940-41, Stretton only [DE 3256/84].

Public Record Office, Kew:
   Whole *County* 1798 [IR.23/70] (see page 9).

Window Tax

None traced.

SHROPSHIRE

Land Tax

Shropshire Records and Research Centre,
Shrewsbury:

1) **Pre-1780:** *Shrewsbury borough,* 1700, 1731, 1740, 1744, 1754, 1763 [3365/281-286]; *Ludlow borough,* 1699, 1700, 1702-80 (incomplete series) [LB8/3/156-240]; *Bridgnorth borough,* 1715; *Clun and Purslow division,* 1775 [3719/6/1-9]; *Stottesden division,* 1728; *Boningale,* 1708, 1719 [3607/2/162,118]; *Buildwas,* 1710 and nd. [2089/5/2/2,3]; *Sheinton,* 1750, 1751 [2089/8/1/1,2]; *Stockton,* 1703-5, 1709, 1718, 1719 [3067/2/34.64,72,164].

2) **1780-1832:** *Shrewsbury borough,* 1780-1, 1784; 1798 [3365/286]; *Clun and Purslow division* 1828 [726/1/31]; *Wenlock franchise,* 1799 [pQE/6/1]; *Stockton,* 1796-1801 and 1803 [3067/2/174-179 and 183]; *Whole County,* 1822 (C19 transcript, location of original unknown) [6001/1883].

3) **Post-1832:** *Clun and Purslow division,* 1832-92; *Ford division,* 1834-58; *Chirbury division,* 1864-89; *Brimstree South division,* 1854, 1862-63; C20 series for most divisions (incomplete).

Detailed lists of LTAs are available for the above at the Centre.

National Library of Wales, *Aberystwyth:*

LTAs for Soughton (par. Llanshilling), 1765, 1771-1774, 1803, 1805 [Powis Castle D&D].

Public Record Office, *Kew:*

Whole County, 1798 [IR.23/71,72] (see page 9).

Window Tax

Shropshire Records and Research Centre, *Shrewsbury:*

Bishops Castle, 1735 [795/19].
Bridgnorth, 1792 [4001/F/8].
Great Ness, 1807/8 [3153/1], 1820/1 [2118/233].
Ludlow (borough), 1696-1787, NC [LB/8/3/85-155].
Shrewsbury (borough), 1698-9, 1710, 1715, 1717, 1729-32, 1751-1752, 1767, 1771-72, 1778-80, 1782-1785 [3365/77,288-300].

National Library of Wales, *Aberystwyth.*

1734-52, Llwyntidmon, Sweeney, Weston Cotton, Abertanat, Bryn, Llyncklis, Measbury, Woolston, Sandford, Aston, Whitington, Frankton, Berghill, Halston, Sutton, West Felton, Rardeston, Rednall, Oldmarton, Ebnal, Hinford, Hisland, Blodwel, Daywell, Ternhill, Henlley and Crickheth [Brogyntyn Rentals and Accounts, D3].

SHROPSHIRE

NORTH BRADFORD
OSWESTRY
PIMHILL
SHREWSBURY
SOUTH BRADFORD
FORD
CHIRBURY
CONDOVER
WENLOCK
BRIMSTREE
B
PURSLOW and CLUN
MUNSLOW
STOTTESDON
L
OVERS
L = LUDLOW
B = BRIDGNORTH

LTA = Land Tax Assessment; M = Many; NC = Near Complete; P = Parishes; S = Some; Y = Years

SOMERSET

Land Tax

Published: *Weston-super-Mare (Winterstoke Hd),* Index: *Part 1, 1766-7; Part 2, 1783-1829; Part 3, 1830-32;* comp. Brian Austin, Woodspring Central Library, 1984.

Somerset Record Office, Taunton:

1) **Pre-1780:** 1759, *Hartcliffe cum Bedminster* and *Portbury Hundreds* only; 1766-7, *all Hundreds, some parishes.*
2) **1780-1832:** *All Hundreds, some years and some parishes.*
3) **Post-1832:** *miscellaneous LTAs.*

LTAs to 1832 are stored in parish/tithing bundles. A detailed catalogue is available.

Public Record Office, Kew,
Whole *County* (but *Bath* is left blank), 1798 [IR.23/73-76] (see page 9).

For BRISTOL, see page 30.

Window Tax

Somerset Record Office, Taunton:

Hundreds:
Kingsbury West and *Milverton* (complete), 1730, 1731, with par. Wilton, 1729 [DD/SF 3889] (500 names).

Parishes:
Ashill, 1700 [D/P/ashl 23/3].
Banwell, 1773-74 [D/P/ban 14/51/1].
Butleigh, 1759 [D/P/butl 4/1/1].
North Curry, 1717 [DD/SF 3114].
Drayton, 1761, 1779 [DD/SAS c1696/6/9/6,9].
Meare, 1795 [D/P/mea 23/2].
Puriton, 1770, 1775-76, 1782 [D/P/pur 20/3/2-3].
Thorne St. Margaret, 1752 [DD/SAS HV33].
Wellow, 1749 [DD/BR/hm 5].
Plus 8 parishes, not detailed, for which there are odd survivals mixed in with QS LTAs.

Wiltshire and Swindon Record Office, Trowbridge:
Long Ashton, 1720 [1178/18/645,648].

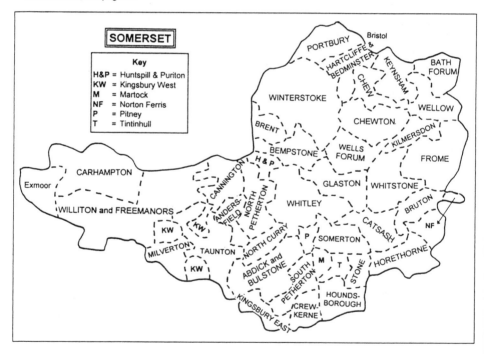

SOMERSET

Key
H&P = Huntspill & Puriton
KW = Kingsbury West
M = Martock
NF = Norton Ferris
P = Pitney
T = Tintinhull

LTA = Land Tax Assessment; M = Many; NC = Near Complete; P = Parishes; S = Some; Y = Years

STAFFORDSHIRE

Land Tax

Staffordshire Record Office, *Stafford:*

1) **Pre-1780:** 1772, *Offlow South Hundred,* only.
   Also: Chillington, 1699, 1704-11 [D590/762-770].
   Cuttlestone, 1719, 1728 [D260/M/E/429/19].
   Wetton, 1731 [D1065/3/1].
   Stowe, n.d. *c.*1750 [D(W)1702/11/1].
2) **1780-1832:** Most years and most places,
   including *Stafford,* arranged by year; no
   survivals for Newcastle; for *Lichfield,* and
   Seisdon Hd.) see below.
   Also Brewood, 1803-48 [D590/772-783];
      1780-1881 [D590/683-4]; 1847 [D590/358].
   Cheadle, 1875 [1245/2].
3) **Post-1832:** 1836-54 SY, *Cuttlestone Hundred.*

Lichfield Record Office, *Lichfield:*

   City and County of Lichfield, 1819 and 1825
   [D25/3/2/5-6]. No other survivals.
   Seisdon Hd., 1799-1846 [D8Z7] (on semi-permanent
loan from **Staffordshire Record Office**).
   Offlow Hd., C20 [D4566].

Public Record Office, *Kew:*
   Whole *County,* 1798 [IR.23/79-81] (see page 9).

Window Tax

Staffordshire Record Office, *Stafford.*

Cuttlestone Hundred, 1711 [D260/M/E/429/19].
Brewood, 1801-06 [D880/5/1].
Fradswell, 1785-87 [D3033/5/3].
Leek Frith, 1704 [D(W)1702/1/12].
Patshull, 1738-59 [D21/A/PZ/9-11].
Stowe, n.d., *c.*1750 [D(W)1702/11/1].

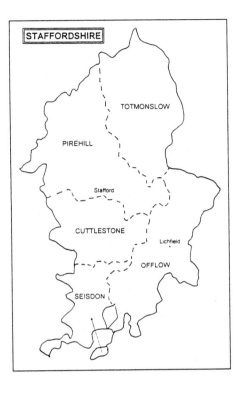

SUFFOLK

Land Tax

Suffolk Record Office (Ipswich Branch), Ipswich:

1) **Pre-1780:** 1707, *Wilford, Colneis* and *Carlford Hundreds*, SP [HA 30:50/22/3,8].
1721-1779, *Ipswich*, MY, SP;
1737, Sternfield (Plomesgate Hundred).
2) **1780-1832:** whole *County*, 1799;
Ipswich, 1780-1806, MY, SP;
Woodbridge division, 1800-32, MY, MP;
Bosmere and Claydon, 1803-32, NC;
Cosford, 1802, SP.
Blything, 1819-32, MY, MP.
3) **Post-1832:** *Hartismere*, 1917-49, MY, MP;
Plomesgate, 1880-1, 1889-90, SP;
Wangford, 1909-49, MY, MP.
Woodbridge division, 1833-90, MY, MP;
Hoxne, 1896-1949, MY, SP;
Bosmere and Claydon, 1833-67, NC;
Dunwich, 1890-1947, NC.
Blything, 1833-1949, MY, MP.
Mutford and Lothingland, 1846-1949, MY, MP.
Colneis, Ipswich & Samford, 1848-1949, MY, MP.

Suffolk Record Office (Bury St. Edmunds Branch), Bury St. Edmunds:

1) **Pre-1780:** *Bury St. Edmunds*, St James, 1770-79;
St. Mary's, 1769, 1772-79.
2) **1780-1832:** *Bury St. Edmunds*, St. James, 1780-1806, St. Mary, 1780-98;
other occasional survivals listed right;
and see above, Ipswich branch, for 1790.
3) **Post-1832:** *Bury St. Edmunds*, 1837-1935, MY;
and occasional survivals listed right.

Division or Hundred
Blackbourne: 2) Badwell Ash, Langham, Bardwell
only, 1829; Hepworth only, 1830.
3) 1923-32, 1946-49, NC;
Walsham only, 1833.
Cosford: 3) 1837, 1883-1945, NC.
Lackford: 3) 1934-36, 1943-49, NC.
Tuddenham only, 1880-91.
Thedwastre: 2) Fornham St. Martin only, 1822.
3) 1858-1949, NC.
Thingoe: 2) Hengrave only, 1820.
3) 1886-1949, NC.

National Library of Wales, Aberystwyth:
Properties in Orford and Sudbury, 1731-2 [Corbett-Winder Deeds and Documents, 3].

Public Record Office, Kew:
Whole *County*, 1798 [IR.23/82-84] (see page 9).

Window Tax

Suffolk Record Office, Ipswich:

1715. Stuston, Redgrave, Burgate, Wyverstone,
Thornham Magna, Rishangles, Thwaite, Thorndon
and Occold [HD 79/AD1/3/9-18].
Ipswich (borough), 1721-89, MY, MP [C10/1/2-113].
Claydon, 1830 [HD 1278/6].
Cotton, 1777 [FB161/A1/5].

Suffolk Record Office, Bury St. Edmunds:

Cosford Hundred, 1802 [K2/6/8] (600 names).
Bury St. Edmunds, St. Mary (parish), 1798-99
[D17/3/2].

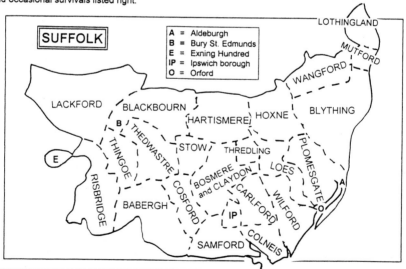

LTA = Land Tax Assessment; M = Many; NC = Near Complete; P = Parishes; S = Some; Y = Years

SURREY

Land Tax

Surrey History Centre, 130 Goldsworth Rd, Woking:

2) **1780-1832**: good coverage, except East Brixton; arranged by place.
3) **Post-1832**: Varying survival, in process of cataloguing, so list below may be subject to revision.

Some LTAs are known to remain in private hands, but these largely duplicate those at *Surrey H.C.*.

Division
Elmbridge: 2) 1780-93, 1795-6, 1798-1832, NC.
3) 1854-1949, MY, MP.
Kingston: 2) 1780-93, 1795-1831, NC.
3) 1854-1946, MY, MP.
West Brixton: 2) 1780-1832, NC.
3) 1934-49, MY, MP.
Godley: 2) 1780-93, 1795-1832, NC.
3) 1946-9, MY, MP.
Wotton: 2) 1780-93, 1795-6, 1798-1831, NC.
3) 1913-4, 1919-20, 1935-49, MY, SP.
Reigate: 1) 1760, Burstow only; 1766, Nutfield only.
2) 1780-93, 1795-1831, NC.
3) 1928-49, MY, MP.
Tandridge: 2) 1780-93, 1795-1832, NC.
3) 1928-49, MY, MP. 1833-45, Titsey only.
Wallington: 2) 1780-93, 1795-1831, NC.
3) 1857-1949, SY, SP.
Copthorne and Effingham:
2) 1780-93, 1795-1832, NC.
3) 1874, 1899, 1904, 1911, 1922-49, MY, MP.
Woking: 2) 1780-93, 1795-6, 1798-1831, NC.
3) 1946-9, SP.
Guildford: 2) 1780-93, 1795-6, 1798-1831, NC.
3) 1935-49, MY, MP.

Blackheath: 2) 1780-93, 1795-6, 1798-1831, NC.
Godalming: 2) 1780-93, 1795-1831, NC.
3) 1892-1949, MY, MP.
Farnham: 2) 1780-93, 1795-1832, NC.
3) 1936-49, MY, MP.
Southwark: 2) 1780-1832, NC.
East Brixton: 2) 1780-1831, MY, SP.

Kingston Museum and Heritage Service:
North Kingston Centre, Richmond Road,
Kingston upon Thames, Surrey KT2 5PE.

Elmbridge: 1751, 1754, SP.
Kingston: 1751 SP; 1751-73, SY, Malden only.

Guildhall Library, Aldermanbury:
Putney, 1704 [MS.230].

London Metropolitan Archives,
40 Northampton Road, London EC1R 0HB:

Third East Brixton Division: Lambeth Dean 1804-24 SY; Christ Church Southwark 1815-24, 1830-34; Clink Liberty 1804-25 MY; Newington 1897-25 MY; Walworth 1808-25 MY; Blackman and Kent Streets 1812-24; all places plus Norwood 1838-1910. Southwark – most divisions: 1798-1910, MY.

Lambeth Archives Dept., Minet Library,
Knatchbull Road, London SE5 9QY:

Chertsey, 1711 [Surrey Deeds 1/2681];
1724, 1725 [Surrey Deeds 1/2690,2692].
Also microfilm of SHC LTAs for Streatham, Tooting, Clapham, Lambeth, Southwark.

Buckinghamshire Record Office, Aylesbury:
Godley, 1935-43, 1946-49; Guildford 1935-43, 1949-50; Staines 1949-50; Woking 1949-50
[all 7/5].

Public Record Office, Kew:
Whole *County*, 1798 [IR.23/85-87] (see page 9).

Window Tax

Surrey History Centre, Woking:

Parishes:
Battersea, 1786 [A9 1/7/h].
Effingham, 1804-12 [G/EFF/19/1-4].
Old Malden, 1756-78, 1823-31 [2473/6/2-8,15-20].
Mortlake, 1779-85 [2397/5/2-9].
Newdigate, 1735-36 [G/NE/4/1].
Shere, 1718 [G/85/20/5].
Thursley, 1785 [QS6/7].

Kingston Museum and Heritage Service:
Kingston (Borough), 1774,1779 [KD8/3/1-2].

Lambeth Archives Department:
Streatham, 1783 [P/S/13/17]; also assessments for taxes on houses and windows, 1800-01 [P/S/13/19].

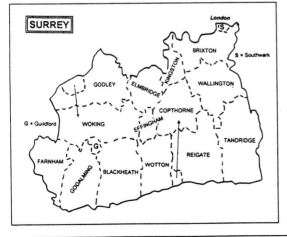

LTA = Land Tax Assessment; M = Many; NC = Near Complete; P = Parishes; S = Some; Y = Years

SUSSEX

Land Tax

Published: *East Sussex Land Tax 1785*, ed. Roger Davey, Sussex R.S. **77**, 1991, £24. *West Sussex* scheduled for publication 1999.

LTAs are split between the *East* and *West Sussex Record Offices*, for the areas covered by each.

East Sussex Record Office, Lewes:

1) **Pre-1780:** *Hastings Rape*, 1693-1779. *Pevensey Rape Upper* and *Lower*, 1750-79. Isolated LTAs for *Hastings, Pevensey Liberty* and *Rye*.
2) **1780-1832:** good coverage for all divisions administered by the County, 1785 for *East Sussex* published, see above. Isolated LTAs for *Hastings, Pevensey Liberty, Rye* and *Winchelsea*.
3) **Post-1832:** considerable survivals.

LTAs to 1832 are arranged by place. Those for *Winchelsea* and *Rye* are amongst their respective town records, and for *Hastings* among the parish records, all at *E.S.R.O.*

Divisions

Hastings Rape: 1) 1693-1779, SY, MP.
2) 1780-1832, NC.
3) 1833-1933, MY, MP.
Hastings Town: 1) All Saints, 1721; St. Mary in the Castle, 1759, 1762.
2) All Saints, 1782, 1784, 1787; St. Clement, 1782-87; St. Mary in the Castle, 1782-90.
Lewes Upper (see also under *W.S.R.O.*):
1) 1703, 1743, one LTA only.
2) 1780-1832, NC.
3) 1833-1948, MY, MP.
Pevensey Rape Lower (see also under *W.S.R.O.*):
1) 1750-79, MY, MP.
2) 1780-1832, NC.
3) 1833-49, 1859, MY, MP.
Pevensey Rape Upper: 1) 1750-79, MY, MP.
2) 1780-1832, NC.
3) 1834-1933, MY, MP.
Pevensey Liberty: 1) 1746, 1771-3.
2) 1788, 1791-6, 1798-1801, 1805, 1809-11, 1815, 1819-21, 1824-9.
3) 1833-49.
Rye: 1) 1711, 1717-8, 1722-3.
2) 1807, 1811-3, 1815, 1817, 1819-20, 1823-4, 1829-31.
Seaford: 3) 1873, 1876, 1878-84, 1886-7, 1889-93, 1895-6, 1901-4, 1916-22, 1925, 1927-33.
Winchelsea: 2) 1785, 1798.
3) 1857-76, MY.

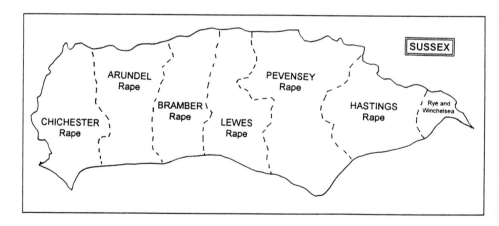

LTA = Land Tax Assessment; M = Many; NC = Near Complete; P = Parishes; S = Some; Y = Years

56

West Sussex Record Office, *Chichester:*
This holds LTAs for the divisions of *Arundel Upper and Lower, Bramber Lower* and *Upper, Chichester Lower* and *Upper, Lewes Lower, Lewes Upper (Clayton, Fulking, Hurstpierpoint, Keymer, Newtimber, Poynings* and *Pycombe;* others in *E.S.R.O.*), and *Pevensey Rape Lower (East Grinstead, Horsted Keynes* and *Linfield;* others in *E.S.R.O.*).

1) **Pre-1780:** 1716. Lindfield [Add.Ms. 39,900];
1750-9, *Pevensey Rape Lower;*
1750-79, East Grinstead, Horsted Keynes,
Lindfield [Add.Mss. 18,419-237].
1753, Petworth [Add.Ms. 1710 and 2734].
2) **1780-1832:** near complete, arranged by place; on microfilm.
3) **Post-1832:** Lewes Lower, 1911-48, SY, MP;
Bramber Upper, 1918-48 SY, SP;
Pevensey Rape Lower, 1833-49, 1859 MY, MP.

Kent County Archives Office, *Maidstone:*
Pevensey Lower: 3) 1942-9, SP.

Public Record Office, *Kew:*
Whole *County,* 1798 [IR.23/88-90] (see page 9).

Window Tax

East Sussex Record Office, *Lewes:*

Divisions:
Hastings Rape (complete except for Northiam, Rye and Winchelsea), 1747 [RF 15/21] (1,870 names).
Pevensey Rape, pars. Chiddingley, Fletching, East Grinstead, Lindfield, Mayfield, Wadhurst, Waldron and Withyham, 1747 [D 472 (LT Misc)] (1,200 names). Both include House Tax.
Pevensey Liberty, 1834 [PEV 520].
Rye, 1722-23 [RYE 84/9,10].
Seaford, 1713 [SEA 644].
Winchelsea, 1799 [WIN 1523].

Parishes:
Ditchling, 1768 [PAR 308 26/1].
Glynde, 1773 [PAR 347 26/3].
Hastings, All Saints, 1782 [PAR 361 26/2];
St. Clement, 1782 [PAR 367 37/2/4].
St. Mary in the Castle, 1782 [PAR 369 26/11].
East Hoathly, 1760, 1766 [PAR 378 37/3/1-3].
Twineham, 1784-85 [HIC 715-6].
Whatlington, 1748 [RF 15/21].

West Sussex Record Office, *Chichester:*

Parishes:
Amberley, 1779 [Add.Ms.12947].
East Grinstead, 1766 [Add.Ms.18419].
Littlehampton, 1737 [Par 127/26/2].
Petworth, 1762 [Add.Ms.2735, photocopy in Add.Ms.1711].

WARWICKSHIRE

Land Tax

Warwickshire County Record Office, *Warwick:*

1) **Pre-1780:** 1775-79 good coverage.
2) **1780-1832:** good coverage.
3) **Post-1832:** considerable survivals.

There are two collections of LTAs:
(a) the Quarter Sessions documents for practically every parish, now arranged by place, generally starting pre-1780 and finishing in 1832 [QS77/1-276];
(b) the later but sometimes overlapping series [CR 863] which is, however, defective geographically.

The survivals can best be described conveniently by grouping the Hundreds into four sets:

A. *Southam, Kirby, Rugby, Kenilworth, Kington Brails, Warwick, Dassett* and *Kineton:*
1) 1774 or 1775 to 1779, all P, NC [QS 77/1].
2) 1780 to 1831 or 1832, all P, NC [QS 77/1].
3) Most parishes, c.1840-c.1936, with Lapworth and Tanworth parishes starting their CR series before 1800.

B. *Barlichway Henley, Barlichway Snitterfield* and *Alcester* - as Set A but the CR 863 series generally starts at 1798.

C. *Barlichway Stratford:*
1) About half the parishes are NC, 1775-1779 (as QS 77/1).
2) All parishes from 1780 or 1798 to 1831 depending on whether their QS 77/1 series has survived [QS 77/1 and/or CR 863].
3) The CR 863 series continues to varying dates spaced out between 1845 and 1946. The only LTAs for Stratford are for 1918-9 (but see *Shakespeare Birthplace,* below).

D. *Coventry* and *Hemlingford Hundreds* (the latter has the divisions of *Birmingham, Tamworth, Solihull and Atherstone*). No CR 863 series LTAs have survived.
1) 1773/4/5. to 1779. Nearly all parishes, NC.
2) 1780-1832. Nearly all P, NC.

Shakespeare Birthplace Trust Record Office, *Stratford-upon-Avon:*

Stratford Borough (High Street and Henley Street only), 1766 [ER 1/107/6];
1822-23 [DR 942/4,5].
Old Stratford, 1776-7 [ER 11/18/2,3, BRU 15/19/88];
1781 [ER 11/18/13];
Fillongley, 1820 [ER 12/35/1];
Little Compton (formerly Glos.), 1797 [ER 13/8/1].

LTA = Land Tax Assessment; M = Many; NC = Near Complete; P = Parishes; S = Some; Y = Years

Warwickshire continued

Coventry City Archives, Coventry:
Coventry wards, 1765-1804 (incomplete).
Ansty 1784-92; Exhall 1772-82; Foleshill 1765-77;
Keresley 1740-86; Radford 1772-85; Stoke 1772-
1786; Styvechale 1772-85; Walsgrave on Sowe
(part) 1772-95; Wyken 1772-92.

Public Record Office, Kew:
Whole County, 1798 [IR.23/91,92] (see page 9).

Window Tax

Warwickshire County Record Office, Warwick:
Ansley, late C18 [CR 300].
Balsall (Hampton), 1746-48, 1799
    [CR 112/149-151,154].
Berkswell, 1775-87 [CR 2237/10].
Brailes, 1700-38 [DR 308/147/1-10].
Hartshill (Mancetter), 1708-37 [N2/570-589].
Kineton, 1813-17 [DR 212/191].
Shustoke, 1789 [CR 1184].
Solihull, 1755-56 [CR 677/4,5].
Southam, n.d. c.1823 [DR 583/175].
Warwick, 1699, 1706-1712 [CR 1612/W18/1,2].
Nether Whitacre, 1766 [DR(B) 3/181].

Birmingham Central Library, Archives Division:
Harborne, 1763, 1784 [DRO 61/13/5/1].
Sheldon, 1790 [DRO 42, box 6, tax returns no.3].

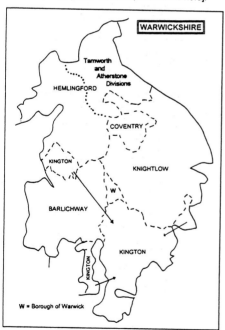

WESTMORLAND

Land Tax

Cumbria Record Office, Kendal:
1) **Pre-1780:** 1765 and/or 1773.
2) **1780-1832:** sparse survivals.
3) **Post-1832:** no survivals.

LTAs are arranged by place.

Ward
Kendal: 1) 1773, all townships except
    Kendal Stramongate, Strickland Roger and
    Strickland Ketal.
  2) 1793, 1809, 1823, 1830-1, most townships.
Lonsdale: 1) 1773, all townships.
  2) 1809, 1823, 1826, 1828, 1830-2, all townships.
East: 1) 1765, 1773, many townships.
  2) 1790, 1823, 1829, many townships.
West: 1) 1765, many townships.
  2) 1809, 1823, 1826, 1831-2, many townships.

Public Record Office, Kew:
Whole County, 1798 [IR.23/93] (see page 9).

Window Tax

Cumbria Record Office, Kendal:
Old Hutton, 1762 [WPR/17].
East and West Wards, 1777. Indexed transcript of
P.R.O. T38/783.

Public Record Office, Kew:
Whole County, 1777 [T38/783,784] (5,449 names).

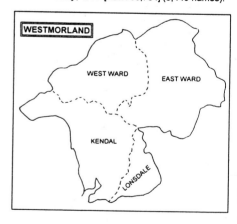

LTA = Land Tax Assessment; M = Many; NC = Near Complete; P = Parishes; S = Some; Y = Years

WILTSHIRE

Land Tax

See 'Land Tax Assessments', Ralph H. Ponting, *Family Tree Magazine*, **9**.4 (Feb. 1993).

Wiltshire and Swindon Record Office, Trowbridge:

1) **Pre-1780:** 1703-52, *Salisbury* (city);
   1773-4, Hundreds of *Bradford, Heytesbury, Melksham, Trowbridge, Warminster* and *Westbury.*
2) **1780-1832:** good coverage.
3) **Post-1832:** many C19 LTAs for Hundreds of *Damerham, Dunworth, Highworth, Melksham* and *Whorlesdown.*

LTAs are arranged by place, and surviving years are listed, parish by parish, in the excellent seven-part series *Location of Documents for Wiltshire Parishes,* compiled and published 1982 by B.J. Carter, 28 Okus Road, Swindon, Wilts. SN1 4JQ, £2 each plus post:

1. Aldbourne to Bromham;
2. Broughton to Dinton;
3. Ditteridge to Hilperton;
4. Hindon to Marlborough;
5. Marston to Rollestone;
6. Rowde to Tockenham;
7. Tollard to Zeals.

Hundreds in Wiltshire are very intermingled. To keep the map simple some enclaves have been omitted.

WILTSHIRE

HIGHWORTH, CRICKLADE and STAPLE
Glos
MALMESBURY
KINGSBRIDGE
N DAMERHAM
CHIPPENHAM
CALNE
SELKLEY
RAMSBURY
BRADFORD
MELKSHAM
POTTERNE & CANNINGS
KINWARDSTONE
SWANBOROUGH
WHORWELLSDOWN
ELSTUB & EVERLEY
WESTBURY
WARMINSTER
HEYTESBURY
AMESBURY
BRANCH & DOLE
UNDER-DITCH
MERE
DUNWORTH
ALDERBURY
W S
CAWDON and CADWORTH
DOWNTON
CHALKE
FRUSTFIELD
S. DAMERHAM

S = Salisbury
W = Wilton

Hundreds:
Alderbury: 2) 1780-1831, NC.
Amesbury: 2) 1780-1832, MP, NC.
   3) 1833-61. Very few.
Branchard Dole: 2) 1780-1831, NC.
   3) Part of Tilshead, 1833-85, MY.
Bradford: 1) 1773-4, MP.
   2) 1780-1831, MP, MY.
   3) 1833, 1880-82, MP.
Calne Hundred and Borough:
   2) 1780, 1782-1831, Complete.
Cawden: 2) 1780-1831, NC.
Chalke: 1) Semley, 1740-79, MY.
   2) 1780-1831, NC.
   3) Three parishes, 1833-76, SY.
Chippenham: 1) Colerne, 1761, 1773
   [at **New College, Oxford,** 3471, 2188].
   2) 1780-1831, NC.
   3) 1840-1940, SP. SY.
Damerham: 2) 1780-1831, All P, NC.
   3) 1833-76, All P, SY.
Devizes Borough: 2) 1780-4, 1786-1831.
Downton: 1) 1740-79, SP, SY.
   2) 1780-1831, MP, MY.
   3) 1833-82, SP, SY.
Dunworth: 2) 1780-1831, NC.
   3) 1833-76, MP, SY.
Elstub and Everley: 2) 1780-1831, MP, MY.
   3) 1833-92. Very few.
Heytesbury: 1) 1773, NC.
   2) 1780-1831, NC.
Highworth: 1) 1700, 1750, SP.
   2) 1780, 1782-1832, MP, MY.
   3) 1833-82, NC.
Kingsbridge: 2) 1780, 1782-1831,
   Complete.
   3) Two parishes, 1833.
Kinwardstone: 2) 1780-1831, NC.
   3) 1875, Complete.
Malmesbury Hundred and Borough:
   2) 1780, 1782-1831, NC.
   3) 1833-70, SP, SY.
Melksham: 1) 1773-4, Complete.
   2) 1780-1831, NC.
   1833-48, All P, SY.
Mere: 2) 1780-1831, Complete.
   3) 1833-76, All P, very few.
Potterne and Canning: 2) 1780-1831,
   Complete.
Ramsbury: 2) 1780-1831, Complete.
Salisbury: 1) 1703-46, NC; 1747-52 SP SY
   [G23/1/182-185].
   2) 1783-1832, SY for St. Martin's parish.
   3) 1837-70, SY for St. Martin's parish and
   Cathedral parish.
Selkley: 2) 1780-1831, MY, MP.
Swanborough: 2) 1780-1831, NC.
Trowbridge (town): 1) 1773-4.
   2) 1780-1811, 1813-31.
   3) 1880-82, 1885.

LTA = Land Tax Assessment; M = Many; NC = Near Complete; P = Parishes; S = Some; Y = Years
---

Wiltshire *continued*

Trustfield: 2) 1781-1831 (two parishes out of three).
3) Landford, 1833.
Underditch: 1) Woodford, 1739.
2) 1780-1832, NC.
Warminster: 1) 1773, MP.
2) 1780-1831, MP, MY.
3) 1837-76, SP, four years.
Westbury: 1) 1773-4, SP.
2) 1780-1831, SP, all years.
3) 1880-2, SP.
Whorlesdown: 2) 1780-1831, Complete.
3) 1833-1923, All P, SY.

Public Record Office, *Kew:*
Whole *County,* 1798 [IR.23/94-96] (see page 9).

Window Tax

Wiltshire and Swindon Record Office,
Trowbridge:

Hundreds:
*Alderbury, Amesbury, Branch and Dole, Cawdon
and Cadworth, Chalk, Downton, Elstub and
Everley, Frustfield* and *Underditch,* 1748;
Alderbury, Amesbury and *Branch and Dole,* 1749
[490/1432] (3,000 names).

Salisbury (City), all four wards, every year 1704-40,
and New Street Ward only, 1741-52
[G23/1/188-191] (600 names per year).

Parishes:
Fonthill Bishop, Hindon and Semley, 1762-74; East
Knoyle, 1771; South Damerham, 1785, and
Winterbourne Monkton, 1787 [A1/344/1-6].
Box, 1752 [878/1].
Calne, 1752 [546/267].
Wroughton, 1768 [1178/18/2].
Fonthill Gifford, 1776 [1855/38].
Salisbury, par. St. Martin, 1784-85 [1899/209].
Charlton, 1785 [1813/39].

Hair Powder Tax

The Hair Powder Tax, Wiltshire, 1796 and 1797, ed.
Beryl Hurley, Wilts. FHS, 1997 [Wiltshire and
Swindon Record Office, WRO A1/395]. Taxpayers
arranged alphabetically under each place.

WORCESTERSHIRE

Land Tax

Worcestershire Record Office, County Hall,
Worcester:
Handlist, arranged by parish, available.

1) **Pre-1780:** no known survivals.
2) **1780-1832:** 1781-1832, MY, MP for all Hundreds
except Worcester City, arranged by year
[Quarter Sessions, Class 152].
3) **Post-1832:** Handlist gives brief details of
survivals for LT Divisions and for individual
parishes.

Hundreds:
(a) Quarter Sessions [Class 152]:

Blakenhurst: 2) 1781, 1787-1831 (gaps), MY, SY.
Doddingtree: 2) 1781, 1787-1831 (gaps, especially
pre-1815), MP, SY.
Lower Halfshire: 1781, 1787-1831 (gaps especially
1797-1804), MP, SY.
Upper Halfshire: 1781-1832 (gaps especially 1782-
1786 and 1793-99), MP, SY.
Middle and *Lower Oswaldslow:* 1781, 1787-1832
(gaps), MP, SY.
East Oswaldslow: 1781-1832 (gaps), MP, SY.
Lower Pershore: 1781-1832 (gaps especially 1795-
1815), MP, SY.
Upper Pershore: 1781-1832 (gaps), MP, SY.

(b) Collector's Duplicates (information re. these has
been incorporated into the handlist mentioned
above):

Ford (parishes of Ashton under Hill, Aston
Somerville, Beckford, Childswickham): 3) 1946-49.
Moreton (parishes of Pebworth, Cow Honeybourne):
3) 1946-49.
Pershore East (formerly *Blakenhurst*):
3) 1923-26, 1946-49, SY, SP.
Pershore West (formerly *Upper Pershore*):
3) 1882-1931, MY, SP.
Stourbridge (formerly *Lower Halfshire*):
3) 1862-1931, MY, SP.
Tewkesbury (parish of Kemerton): 3) 1946-49.
Upton Division (formerly *Lower Pershore*):
2) 1830-1832, SP.
3) 1833-1941, MY, SP.
Worcester City Division: 2) 1817-1832, MY, MP.
3) 1833-1936, MY, SP.
Middle and *Lower Oswaldslow* (late *Worcester*):
2) 1797-1832, MY, SP.
3) 1833-1946, MY, SP.

***The Shakespeare Birthplace Trust Record
Office,*** *Stratford-upon-Avon:*
Abbots Norton, 1795 [DR 5/1917].

LTA = Land Tax Assessment; M = Many; NC = Near Complete; P = Parishes; S = Some; Y = Years

Public Record Office, Kew:
Whole County, 1798 [IR.23/97,98] (see page 9).

(see page 9).

Window Tax

Worcestershire Record Office,
St. Helen's Branch, Worcester:

Parishes:
Inkberrow, 1801, and Feckenham, 1827 [705.89:
BA 1016/22].
Ripple, 1763 [850: BA 348/5].

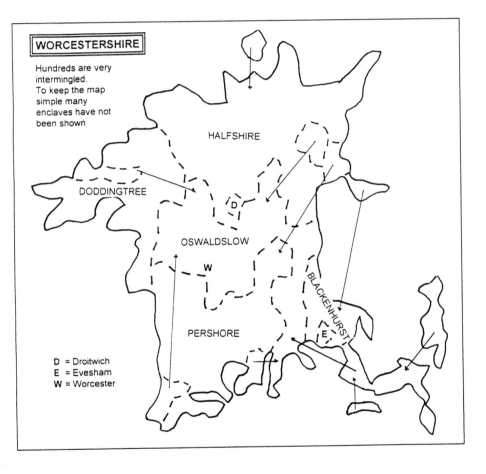

WORCESTERSHIRE

Hundreds are very
intermingled.
To keep the map
simple many
enclaves have not
been shown

HALFSHIRE

DODDINGTREE

D

OSWALDSLOW

W

BLACKENHURST

PERSHORE

E

D = Droitwich
E = Evesham
W = Worcester

LTA = Land Tax Assessment; M = Many; NC = Near Complete; P = Parishes; S = Some; Y = Years

YORKSHIRE

Male Servants' Tax, 1780

Published: J.J. Cartwright, 'List of persons in York-shire who paid tax on male servants in 1780', *York-shire Archaeological Journal,* **14** (1896), pp. 65-80.

YORKSHIRE: EAST RIDING, YORK and AINSTY

Land Tax

East Riding of Yorkshire Archive Office, Beverley:

East Riding

1) **Pre-1780:** few survivals, in private hands.
2) **1780-1832:** 1782 or 1783, 1787-1830, 1832, NC, for all Wapentakes except Beverley cum Membris and Hull County (missing years shown below), arranged by place.
3) **Post-1832:** C20 only, shown below, and see *York City Archives,* below.

A prior appointment to consult records at the *East Riding of Yorkshire A.O.* is essential.

Wapentakes (for 1780-1832 see also above):
Bainton Beacon: 3) 1934-49, NC.
Beverley cum Membris: 2) 1790-96, 1802, 1805, NC.
Buckrose: 3) 1934-39, NC.
Dickering: 1) Over 40 parishes/townships (104 docs.), *c.*1730-*c.*1753 [DDX 327].
   3) 1925-6, 1928-9, 1930-1, 1934-49, NC.
Harthill: 3) Pocklington Poor Law Union, parochial LTA book *c.*1904 [PLU records].
Holderness, Middle: 3) 1921-41, NC.
Holderness, North: 2) includes 1831.
   3) 1932-1940, NC.
Holderness, South: 3) 1891-1941, NC.
Holme Beacon: 2) missing 1787, 1798.
   3) 1929-49, NC.
Hunsley Beacon: 3) 1931-40 (North); 1917-40 (South).
Hull County: 1) Anlaby and Wolfreton (8 docs.) 1715-65 [DDBL 1].
   2) no survivals.
   3) 1922-41, NC.
Ouse and Derwent: 3) 1929-49, NC; see also *York City Archives,* below.
Wilton Beacon: 2) missing 1832.

York City Archives Dept., York:

County of the City of York
York city:
1) Holy Trinity King's Court, 1757.
2) St. Helen's (parish), *c.*1825; St. John del Pike, 1826, 1828-30;
3) 1906-50, SY, SP; 1898-9, St.Olave Marygate.
Ainsty: 3) 1885-6, MP, 1916-7, SP.

York City Archives: East Riding
Ouse and Derwent Wapentake:
   3) 1898-9, NC.

Kingston-upon-Hull City Record Office, Hull:
Town and county of Kingston upon Hull, 1773, 1782, 1791, 1796, 1799, 1823, 1840 [DMX268].
Hull and Myton, 1798.

John Goodchild Collection, Wakefield
(see page 65).
Bridlington, 1738.

Public Record Office, Kew:
   East Riding, 1798 [IR.23/99,100]; *City of York* and Hull, 1798 [IR.23/110] (see page 9).

Window Tax

York City Archives Department, York:
York (City), 19 parishes, 1701 [K96] (650 names).

The Borthwick Institute of Historical Research, York:
   Riccall (parish), 1735 [PR/RIC 140].

Kingston-upon-Hull City Record Office, Hull:
Kingston-upon-Hull: Town and County (complete), 1774, 1779; (part) 1778 [CT 102-140].

East Riding of Yorkshire Archive Office, Beverley:
Parish: Wansford, 1759 [DDX 327].

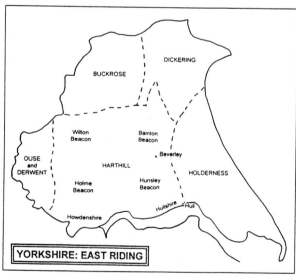

YORKSHIRE: EAST RIDING

LTA = Land Tax Assessment; M = Many; NC = Near Complete; P = Parishes; S = Some; Y = Years

YORKSHIRE: NORTH RIDING

Land Tax

North Yorkshire County Record Office,
Northallerton:

1) **Pre-1780:** good coverage for surviving years in six Wapentakes.
2) **1780-1832:** good coverage except Rydale pre-1801.
3) **Post-1832:** LTAs are unsorted, unlisted and unavailable.

LTAs to 1832 are arranged by year.

Wapentakes

Allertonshire: 1) 1774, NC.
  2) 1781-1832, NC.
Birdforth: 1) 1692-5, 1699, 1712-65, NC.
  2) 1781-1810, 1816-30, NC
Bulmer: 2) 1781-1832, NC.
  3) 1898-9, SP.
Gilling East: 1) 1770-6, NC.
  2) 1781-1807, 1809-32, NC.
Gilling West: 1) 1769-74, 1778, NC.
  2) 1781-98, 1800-7, 1810-2, 1816, 1819, 1820, 1823-32, NC.
Hallikeld: 2) 1781-1829, 1831, NC.
Hang East: 1) 1769.2) 1781-1831, NC.
Hang West: 1) 1759-60, 1769, NC.
  2) 1781-1801, 1805-7, 1809-12, 1816, 1818-31, NC.
Langbaurgh East: 1781-98, 1806-7, 1815, 1817-32, NC.

Langbaurgh West: 2) 1781-99, 1801-5, 1814-6, 1819-26, 1828-32, NC.
Pickering East and West:
  2) 1781-98, 1800-7, 1809-32, NC.
Rydale: 2) 1801-7, 1809-10, 1812-32, NC.
Whitby Strand: 2) 1781-92, 1794, 1798, 1806, 1812, 1816-32, NC.

Boroughs

Richmond: 1) 1700-1780 (some 50 years, in poor condition).
  2) 1780-1804 SY.
Scarborough: 1) 1765.

***West Yorkshire Archive Service, Leeds District Archives,** Leeds.*
  Clifton township, 1741 [NH 2588 B].
***Durham County Record Office,** Durham.*
  Craike: 1759-60, 1829 [Q/D/L 162].

***Public Record Office,** Kew.*
  North Riding, 1798 [IR.23/101-103] (see page 9).

Window Tax

North Yorkshire County Record Office,
Northallerton:

Parishes
Clapham, 1784, 1803, 1809 [PR/CPM/14/1,2,3 and MIC 1179].
Kilburn, 1802-19, 1822-23, 1828-30 [PR/KLB/13/3/1-20, and 13/4/1-2, and MIC 1876].

***Teesside Archives Department,** Middlesbrough:*
  Kirkleatham (parish), n.d., c.1790 [PR/KRL/11/25].

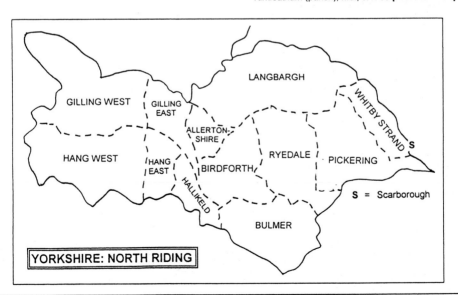

YORKSHIRE: NORTH RIDING

LANGBARGH

GILLING WEST
GILLING EAST
ALLERTON-SHIRE
WHITBY STRAND
S
HANG WEST
HANG EAST
BIRDFORTH
RYEDALE
PICKERING
HALLIKELD
S = Scarborough
BULMER

YORKSHIRE: NORTH RIDING

LTA = Land Tax Assessment; M = Many; NC = Near Complete; P = Parishes; S = Some; Y = Years

63

YORKSHIRE: WEST RIDING

Land Tax

West Yorkshire Archive Service, *Wakefield:*

The bulk of LTAs for the West Riding are held in this archive office, detailed catalogue available; but see also holdings at *Doncaster, Leeds, Bradford, Sheffield* and the *John Goodchild Collection.*

1) **Pre-1780:** 1750-79 Wakefield townships only; otherwise isolated survivals. LTAs for *Staincross Wapentake* 1692-1728 are at *Bradford Archives.*
2) **1780-1832:** very comprehensive coverage, within wapentakes arranged by township.
3) **Post-1832:** C19 *Lower Agbrigg* only; some C20 LTAs for other divisions. See also *Leeds*, right.

The *W.Y.A.S.* publishes a *Search Guide to the English Land Tax*, by R.W. Unwin, 1982, £2.50. This describes how the LT worked, gives examples and facsimilies, and makes suggestions for its use in research. However, it does not itself list the LTA holdings either at the W.Y.A.S. or elsewhere.

Wapentake
Agbrigg (Wakefield townships only):
1) 1752, 1754-5, 1757-60, 1763, 1765-8, 1770-80, SY missing for some townships.
See also *John Goodchild Collection*, right.
Agbrigg (all townships): 2) 1781-5, 1787-1805, 1807-15, 1817-32, NC.
Agbrigg (Lower): 3) 1850, 1855, 1860-1, 1865-6, 1870-1, 1875-6, 1880-1, 1890-1, 1895-6, 1900, 1901, 1905-6, 1910-1, 1915-6, 1920-1, 1925-6, 1930-1, 1935-6, 1945-6.
Barkston Ash: 2) 1781-6, 1788-97, 1799-1815, 1817-28, 1830-32, NC ;
Upper only: 1798, 1829.
3) 1908-9, 1911-20, 1925-6, 1929-30, 1933-4, 1944-9.
Claro: 2) 1781-6, 1788-92, 1794-8, 1800-15, 1817-1821, 1823-7, 1829-32, NC.
Lower only: 1793, 1819, 1822;
Upper only: 1828.
3) see also *Leeds*, right.
Morley: 2) 1781-6, 1788-1815, 1817-32, NC.
2 & 3) see also *Leeds*, right.
Osgoldcross: 2) 1781-6, 1788, 1790-99, 1801-2, 1804-6, 1808-15, 1817-32, NC.
Upper only: 1789, 1803; *Lower* only: 1807.
Skyrack: 1) 1753.
2) 1781-6, 1788-1813, 1815, 1817-1818, 1820-23, 1825-32, NC.
Upper only: 1789, 1819;
Lower only: 1824.
2 & 3) see also *Leeds*, right.
Staincliffe with Ewcross: 1) 1760.
2) 1782-86, 1788-1806, 1808-15, 1817-28, 1830-1832, NC.
East only: 1829; *West* only: 1781, 1807.

Staincross: 1) see *Bradford*, page 65.
2) 1781-6, 1788-9, 1791-93, 1795-1800, 1802-9, 1811-5, 1817-21, 1823, 1825-8, 1830-2, NC.
Upper only: 1801, 1824;
Lower only: 1794, 1810.
3) 1934-5, 1939-40, 1943-9.
Strafforth and Tickhill: 2) 1780-6, 1788-1815, 1817-1823, 1825-32, NC.
Upper only: 1824.
3) 1939-50.
Liberty of Ripon: 2) 1781-1832, NC (but lacking most parts for 1786).

Doncaster Archives Department, *Doncaster:*

1) 1702-03, *Soke of Doncaster*, SP;
1700, 1703, 1710, 1712, 1775-79, Doncaster township only;
1712, Blaxton only;
1779, Hexthorpe only;
1751-79, Kirk Sandall only (Strafforth and Tickhill wapentake).
2) 1792-1808, *Soke of Doncaster*, NC;
1780-84, 1786-91, 1809, 1811, Doncaster township only;
1780-91, Hexthorpe with Balby only;
1801-32, *Strafforth and Tickhill wapentake*, MY, MP; 1780-93, Kirk Sandall only.
3) 1833-1926, *Strafforth and Tickhill wapentake*, MY, MP.

West Yorkshire Archives Service, Leeds District Archives, *Leeds:*

2) Harewood Estate, 1806; 1794-1810 - a few earlier LTAs for certain wapentakes.
Claro: 2) 1799 S [DB227].
3) 1923-1949 [Acc 1165].
Ewecross: 2) 1790-1803 SY [DB227].
Leeds: 2) 1808 [DB227].
3) 1837-1949 [Acc 1077].
Liberty of Ripon: 2) 1798-1812 SY [DB227].
Lower Strafforth and Tickhill: 2) 1798-1812 SY [DB227].
Morley: 2) 1798-1812 SY [DB227].
2 & 3) 1805-1949 [Acc 1161].
Skyrack: 2) 1803-1809 SY [DB227].
2 & 3) 1830-1949 [Acc 1077].
Staincliffe: 2) 1798-1809 SY [DB227].
Staincross: 2) 1798-1813 SY [DB227].

John Goodchild Collection, *Local History Study Centre, below Central Library, Wakefield* (available by appointment by letter, only. No photocopying):

1) Wakefield township, SY from 1740s.
2 & 3) *Wapentake of Lower Agbrigg*, 1787,1829-60.

LTA = Land Tax Assessment; M = Many; NC = Near Complete; P = Parishes; S = Some; Y = Years

Yorkshire: West Riding continued

Bradford Archives Department, Bradford:

1) *Staincross Wapentake,* 1692; 1693 (Cawthorn
   Bill only);1696; 1701-28, SY, SP [SpST
   Collection 2352-3, 2356, 2363].
   Elland and Greetland, 1702 [MM79].
   Heaton, 1765 [JOW]; 1767 [HOD].
   Malham, 1746 [MM81].
   Eccleshill, 1705-08 [DB5 C8-24].
   Tong, 1704 (transcript), 1760 [TONG].
1 & 2) Shelf, 1763-1808 [MM75].
2 & 3) Malham, 1827-34 [MM81].
   Tong, 1795-1861 [TONG].

Sheffield Archives.

1) Barnoldswick 1756-7, 1759-60, 1770 [OD 1178].
   Beighton 1700, 1704, 1709-10, 1764 [MD 5787].
   Eccleshall 1772 [WWM Br P109].
   Ecclesfield 1740 [SC451].
   Fenwick 1712 [BFM 39].
   Pontefract 1693, 1707, 1711, 1719, 1729-30
   [BFM 38].
   Waldershelf 1774 [MD 6266/23].
   Worsbrough 1738-1799, MY [EM 1002].
   Wortley 1768 [Wh M 57/1-2].
2) Brimington 1793 [OD 1553/12].
   Carlton 1780 [Wh M10].
   Norton 1801 [Fr C 75], 1810 [MD 3822/5].
   Thurlstone 1802-03 [WBC 47].
3) *South Yorkshire* 1836-1899, MY, MP
   [LD267-313].

Public Record Office, Kew:
West Riding, 1798 [IR.23/104-09]
(see page 9).

Window Tax

**Borthwick Institute of Historical
Research,** York:

Selby (parish), 1756, 1760, 1773,
1782, 1785, 1788 (incl. Shop
Tax), 1789 [PR/SEL 307-308,
343-346].

Bradford Archives Department,
Bradford:

Horsforth, 1766 [Sp.St/11/8/1/49].
Tong, n.d. c.1823-4 [Tong 11e/67
and 12k/19].

Calderdale District Archives, Halifax:
Elland-cum-Greetland (township in par. Halifax),
1725 [EG/A/33].
Sowerby (t'ship in par. Halifax), 1758-69 [SPL:153].

Doncaster Archives Department, Doncaster:
Various townships, 1700-12 [AB 6/2/10].
Doncaster (Borough), 1780-82, 1788-93
[AB 6/2/13-21].
Parishes: Kirk Sandall, 1750-93 [P13/6/A/1].
Swinton, 1764-1834, NC [P59/6/E/1/1,2].
Thorne, 1798-99 [PR.Tho.24].
Wadworth, 1825, 1828 [P21/6/E/1/1,2].

Leeds District Archives, Leeds:
Carleton in Craven, 1757-58, 1760, 1763-65, 1767-
1770 [P18/173,177].
Birstwith (township in par. Hampsthwaite), 1778
[P12/70].
Kippax, 1760, 1798-99, 1818, 1821-23
[P47/116,118,122-125].

Yorkshire Archaeological Society Library, Leeds:
Selby (parish), 1755 [MD 186].

Sheffield Archives.
Barnoldswick 1756-57, 1760, 1770 [OD 1178].
Beighton 1764 [MD 5787/3].
Carlton 1780 [Wh M 10].
Eccleshall 1725 [WWM Br P 110].
Ecclesfield 1738, 1740 [SC 449-450].
Waldershelf 1774 [MD 6266/23].
Wortley 1768 [Wh M 57/3].

   None traced at **Wakefield H.Q.** and **Kirklees
Archives.**

YORKSHIRE: WEST RIDING

STAINCLIFFE CLARO Ainsty of YORK SKYRACK BARKSTON ASH MORLEY OSGOLDCROSS AGBRIGG STAINCROSS STRAFFORTH and TICKHILL

LTA = Land Tax Assessment; M = Many; NC = Near Complete; P = Parishes; S = Some; Y = Years

SCOTLAND

Scottish Record Office, *Edinburgh:*

Land Tax

Midlothian, 1799-1812 [E327 and E920].

Window Tax

Burghs:
Whole of *Scotland* (arranged in alphabetical sequence, in chronological volumes), coverage the same as for respective counties (below), 1748 for some, 1753-98 for most (1796 missing for all) [E326/1/126-218].

Counties:
(arranged by districts within counties in chronological volumes):
Aberdeenshire, 1753-95, 1797-98 [E326/1/1-6].
Angus (co. Forfar), 1748, 1753-95, 1797-98 [E326/1/50-53].
co. Argyll, 1748, 1753-95, 1797-98 [E326/1/7-10].
co. Ayr, 1753-95, 1797-98 [E326/1/11-16].
co. Banff, 1748, 1753-95, 1797-98 [E326/1/17-18].
co. Berwick, 1748, 1753-95, 1797-98 [E326/1/19-23].
Bute (Isle of), 1753-95, 1797-98 [E326/1/24].
Caithness, 1748, 1753-95, 1797-98 [E326/1/25-26].
co. Clackmannan, 1748, 1753-95, 1797-98 [E326/1/27-28].
co. Cromarty, 1748, 1753-95, 1797-98 [E326/1/29 and 108].
co. Dumbarton, 1748, 1753-95, 1797-98 [E326/1/30-31]
co. Dumfries, 1748, 1753-95, 1797-98 [E326/1/32-36].
co. Fife, 1748, 1753-95, 1797-98 [E326/1/42-49].
co. Inverness, 1748, 1753-59, 1770-95, 1797-98 [E326/1/54-55].
co. Kincardine, 1753-95, 1797-98 [E326/1/56-57].
co. Kinross, 1748, 1753-95, 1797-98 [E326/1/58].
co. Kirkcudbright, 1748, 1753-95, 1797-98 [E326/1/59-61].
co. Lanark, 1753-95, 1797-98 [E326/1/62-70].
East Lothian, 1748, 1753-95, 1797-98 [E326/1/37-41].
Midlothian, 1748, 1753-95, 1797-98 [E326/1/71-90].
West Lothian, 1753-95, 1797-98 [E326/1/121-22].
Moray (co. Elgin), 1753-95, 1797-98 [E326/1/91-92].
co. Nairn, 1753-95, 1797-98 [E326/1/54 and 93].
Orkney (Isles of), 1759-95, 1797-98 [E326/1/94].
co. Peebles, 1753-95, 1797-98 [E326/1/95-96].
Perthshire, 1748, 1753-95, 1797-98 [E326/1/97-102].
co. Renfrew, 1753-95, 1797-98 [E326/1/103-107].
co. Ross, 1748, 1753-95, 1797-98 [E326/1/108-110].
co. Roxburgh, 1748, 1753-95, 1797-98 [E326/1/111-115].

co. Selkirk, 1753-95, 1797-98 [E326/1/116].
Shetland (Isles of), 1759-95, 1797-98 [E326/1/125].
co. Stirling, 1748, 1753-95, 1797-98 [E326/1/117-119].
co. Sutherland, 1748, 1753-95, 1797-98 [E326/1/108 and 120].
co. Wigtown (Galloway), 1748, 1753-95, 1797-98 [E326/1/123-124].

Assessed Taxes

For the whole of *Scotland* (arranged by district within counties and separately by burghs, in chronological bundles).

Inhabited House Tax, 1778-98 [E326/3/1-64].
Commutation Taxes (additional duties on houses and windows), 1784-98 [E326/2/1-57].
Shop Tax, 1785-89 [E326/4/1-8].
Female Servants Tax, 1785-92 [E326/6/1-28].
Horse Tax (carriage and saddle horses), 1785-98 [E326/9/1-33].
Farm Horse Tax (workhorses and mules), 1797-98 [E326/10/1-13].
Dog Tax, 1797-98 [E326/11/1-2].
Clock and Watch Tax, 1797-98 [E326/12/1-2].
Aid and Contribution Tax, co. Peebles only, 1798-1799 [E326/13/1].
Income Tax, 1799-1802 [E326/14/1-2].

Property Valuations

From 1855 on the **Scottish Record Office** has a complete series of annual Valuation Rolls covering by location every piece of property in Scotland. These give names of proprietors, tenants and occupiers.

As shown above, Land Tax Assessments in Scotland only survive for Midlothian. However, the information that can be gathered from the Land Tax records in England and Wales in earlier years can in Scotland be found much more readily and comprehensively in the General, Particular and Burgh Registers of Sasines, and in the Register of Deeds, dating from the 16th century.

IRELAND

Sir Richard Griffiths' *Primary Valuation of Rateable Property in Ireland*, 1848-64, arranged by county and barony, names each occupier or tenant, with townland or city location, area of holding and valuation assessment.

This is printed in over 200 volumes, to be found in only a few major libraries, but also available on microfiche. The **Society of Genealogists** has **Indexes** to the Valuation and the 'Tithe Applotment Books'.

WALES

Microfilm copies of the **1798** LTas [P.R.O. IR.23] for the Welsh counties (excluding Flintshire but including Monmouthshire) are available at the *National Library of Wales* [NLW Films 900-3].

ANGLESEY

Land Tax

Anglesey County Record Office, Llangefni:

LTAs are arranged by place.

Hundreds of Menai and Tindaethwy:
1) **Pre-1780:** c.1744/53-1779, SY, MP; some as early as 1712.
2) **1780-1832:** SY, MP.
3) **Post-1832:** to 1917, 1934-49, SY, MP.
Hundreds of Malltraeth, Llifon, Talybolion and Twycelyn:
1) **Pre-1780:** c.1744/53-1799, SY, SP.
2) **1780-1832:** 1780-1814, SY, SP.
3) **Post-1832:** 1934-49, SY, MP.

National Library of Wales, Aberystwyth:

Hundred of Talybolion: 1) 1693-4, 1706, 1709 [Carreglwyd 981, 1191, 258, 221].
Beaumaris, 133 [NLW MS.1550F].

Department of Manuscripts, Main Library, University of Wales, Bangor.
Llangefni: 1792-94, 1853 [9514-9518].

Public Record Office, Kew:
Whole *County*, 1798 [IR.23/111] (see page 9).

Window Tax

Anglesey County Record Office, Llangefni:

Anglesey, 1751-65, SY, MP;
also Llanfairmathafarneithaf, 1719, and Llandegfan, 1774, 1786 [WQT/80-142].

National Library of Wales, Aberystwyth:
Llanfigel, 1703-04 [Carreglwyd Colln., 2241].

BRECONSHIRE

Land Tax

National Library of Wales, Aberystwyth:

1) **Pre-1780:** 18 parishes, mainly in *Hundreds of Merthyr* and *Defynnog*, 1734, 1754, 1760-2, 1766, 1771, 1773-4, 1777-8 [Penpont Deeds and Documents].

Breconshire continued

2) **1780-1832:** 1780, 1787, as above;
1806, *Crickhowell Hundred* [Maybery Collection];
1817, *Builth and Pencelli Hundreds*;
1825-6, *Builth and Talgarth Hundreds* [both in Cefnbryntalch Collection].
Note. No Quarter Sessions series.

Public Record Office, Kew:
Whole *County*, 1798 [IR.23/112] (see page 9).

Window Tax

National Library of Wales, Aberystwyth:

Merthyr Hundred, 1761-63, 1768, 1778, 1780, 1787;
Devynock (or Defynnog) Hundred, 1747, 1771, 1781 [both Penpont (1936) Mss. nos. 1896-2122].

CAERNARVONSHIRE

Land Tax

Caernarfon Record Office, Caernarfon:

1) **Pre-1780:** 1746-8, 1750-1, 1760-1, 1769-79, SP.
2) **1780-1832:** varying survival, most for 1792-8, 1810, some 1782-91 [Quarter Sessions records, XQA/LT], arranged by place. Note also those at the *University of Wales, Bangor*, page 68.
3) **Post-1832:** C20, post-1933 only, subject to a 30-year rule [Inland Revenue Collector's Office].

Hundred or Commote
Arllechwedd Isaf (Conwy area):
1) 1746-8, 1750-1, 1760-1, 1775-6, NC.
2) 1792-7, 1810, NC.
3) 1935-42, MY, SP.
Arllechwedd Uchaf (Llanfairfechan area):
1) 1746-8, 1750-1, 1761, 1775-6, NC.
2) 1792-8, 1810, 1812, NC.
3) 1933-49, MY, MP.
Creuddyn (Llandudno area):
1) 1746-8, 1750-1, 1761, 1775-6, NC.
2) 1792-8, 1810, NC.
3) 1935-42, Llysfaen (now Conwy) only.
Cymydmaen (Aberdaron area):
2) 1782-4, 1787-9, 1791-2, 1794-5, 1797, 1800-1, 1803-15, 1817-9, NC.
3) 1935-49, NC.
Dinllaen (Nefyn area):
1) 1767, Abererch only.
2) 1782-91, 1793-8, 1800-19, NC.
3) 1935-49, NC.

LTA = Land Tax Assessment; M = Many; NC = Near Complete; P = Parishes; S = Some; Y = Years

Caernarvonshire *continued*

Eifionydd (Criccieth and Porthmadog area):
1) 1769-71, SY, SP. One year preserved for most parishes.
2) 1784-5, 1789-90, 1794-8, 1800-8, 1810-4, 1817-20, NC.
3) 1935-49, NC.
Gafflogion (Pwllheli area):
2) 1782-5, 1787-9, 1791, 1793, 1795-8, 1800-14, 1817-8, MY, MP.
3) 1935-49, NC.
Is-gwyrfai (Bangor and Caernarfon area):
1) 1770-79, NC;
1761, Beddgelert (Lordship of Nantgwynant).
2) 1780-4, 1788-9, 1792-5, 1801-13, 1815-22, 1825-30, NC.
3) 1933-49, NC.
Nantconwy (Betws-y-coed area):
1) 1746-8, 1761, 1775-6, NC.
2) 1792-3, 1795-7, 1810, 1812, NC.
3) 1935-42, NC.
Uwchgwyrfai (Pen-y-groes area):
1) 1770-5, 1777-9, NC.
2) 1780-4, 1788-90, 1792-5, 1801-13, 1815-22, 1825-30, NC.
3) 1935-49, NC.

Department of Manuscripts, Main Library, University of Wales, *Bangor.*
Many LTAs for various parishes are extant in the Porth-yr-Aur collection [4050-4124], dating from 1768 to 1828, which fill in various gaps in the Quarter Sessions records. These are, notably:
1) 1700-49: Llanbedr-y-Cennin [F.B. 8172];
1768, 1770: Llanfairfechan;
1772: Llanllechid.
2) 1783: Many parishes;
1784, 1793, 1813-14, 1826: Llanwnda [9746];
1788: Llandwrog [9747];
1789: Eifionydd and Uwchgwyrfai, MP;
1802: Cymydmaen, Dinllaen and Gafflogion, MP;
1824: Isgwyrfai and Uwchgwyrfai, MP.
2 & 3) 1827-36, 1853-1930: *Caernarvonshire,* Complete (except for 1908-9, SP) [8554-8591].
1836-37: Aberdarn [10470-1].

National Library of Wales, *Aberystwyth.*
Carnarvon (town and liberties), 1718, 1721, 1727 [Nanharan Deeds and Documents, 184-6].
Llandudwen, 1772 [Llanfair & Brynodol DD, MS.12].
Uchgorfai [Uwchgwyrfail] and *Isgorfai* [Is-gwyrfail] hundreds, 1783 [NLW MS. 1687B].
Llanwnda, 1783-4, 1813-14, 1826 [ts copies, NLW MS. 11899C].

Public Record Office, *Kew:*
Whole *County,* 1798 [IR.23/115] (see page 9).

Window Tax

Caernarfon Record Office, *Caernarfon:*
Aber (parish), 1775 [X/pa ABER/497].

CARDIGANSHIRE

Land Tax

National Library of Wales, *Aberystwyth:*

2 & 3) **1780-1871:** *Cardiganshire.* Complete *County,* some substantial gaps [Roberts & Evans Papers, 55/1-66/34, working list now available].
Ucha yn Dre and Issa yn Dre (Generglyn hd.), 1800 [Nanteos Ms & Docs, preliminary schedule].
Aberystwyth (town and liberty), 1816 [Cymerau DD].
Cilcennin, 1885 [E. Ben Morus corres, Pen-wern D].
Forty parishes, 1915-26.

Public Record Office, *Kew:*
Whole *County,* 1798 [IR.23/113] (see page 9).

CARMARTHENSHIRE

Land Tax

Carmarthenshire Record Office, *Carmarthen:*

Whole *County,* 1798 [mf. of PRO IR.23/114].
Most of *County:* 1930, 1935 [Trant Collection].

Divisions:
Cayo/Caeo: 1928 [Glasbrook Collection].
Kidwelly/Cydweli: 1912-18 [T/IR].
Perfedd: 1914, 1916-17 [Acc 4154-4171];
1926, 1928 [Glasbrook Box 52];
1946-49 [Acc 4283-4300].

Parishes:
Llangennech 1729 [DX 114/3].
Berwick (Llanelli) 1730, 1766-7 [DX 114/4,8-9].
Newchurch 1768 [Cwmgwili 789].
Llandilo 1844 [Derwydd D1 146].
Copies of originals at NLW: Cwmtwrch (Caeo par.) 1817; Caeo hamlet (Caeo hd.) 1824; Dyffryn Cyduch (Perfedd hd.) 1824 [Accs 1605-07].

Llanelli Public Library:
Llanelly Borough, 1776.
Llangennech (parish), 1806.
Commote of Carnwallon, 1801.
Llanelly (parish), 1807.
Glyn (hamlet), 1810.

National Library of Wales, *Aberystwyth:*
Mothvey, 1797 [D.T.M. Jones, Llandovery, 2445].
Cwmtwrch and Caio (Lower) hamlets , par. Caio, and hamlet of Dyffrin Cydrich, Perfeth hd., 1817-24 [NLW Misc. Records 144-50].

Public Record Office, *Kew:*
Whole *County,* 1798 [IR.23/114] (see page 9).

Window and Assessed Taxes

Llanelli Public Library:
Llanelly (borough and hamlet), 1807-8 (also horse and carriage tax returns etc.).

LTA = Land Tax Assessment; M = Many; NC = Near Complete; P = Parishes; S = Some; Y = Years
---

DENBIGHSHIRE

Land Tax

Denbighshire Record Office, Ruthin:

1) **Pre-1780:** 1747-79, SY, SP.
2) **1780-1832:** 1780-1800, 1825-31, SY, MP.
3) **Post-1832:** C20 LTAs only.

LTAs are arranged by place.

Hundreds/Divisions
Bromfield: 1) 1759-60, SP; 1778-9, NC.
  2) 1780-96, NC; 1798, SP.
  3) 1915-48, NC.
Chirk: 1) 1758-9, SP.
Lower Chirk: 2) 1781-2, 1784, 1794, 1798-1800,
  SP.
Upper Chirk: 2) 1782, 1784, 1786-7, 1789-1792,
  1794-6, 1825-31, SP.
Cynlleth: 3) 1936-49, NC.
Isaled: 1) 1760, SP; 1754 Llanfair T.H. only.
  2) 1782-98, 1825-30, SY, SP.
  3) 1933-52, NC.
Isdulas: 1) 1747, 1749, 1754, 1759-61, SP.
  2) 1825-9, NC.
Nantheudwy: 3) 1936-49, NC.
Ruthin: 1) 1760-1, SP.
  2) 1797-8, 1829-31, SY, SP.
  3) 1933-52, NC.
Uwchdulas: 3) 1934-56, NC.
Uwchmynydd: 3) 1938-49, NC.
Yale: 1) 1759-61, SP.
  2) 1793, 1796-7, NC.

Flintshire Record Office, Hawarden:
Wrexham (town): 1) 1721 [D/E/673].

National Library of Wales, Aberystwyth:
Llandysilio, 1690, 1707, 1742, 1794, 1800 [Harrison
  Deeds and Documents, Box 12/9].
Glynfechan (Llansanffraid Glyn Ceiriog), 1703-6,
  1778 [Wenniar Documents 27-8,30,38].
Several townships, 1738, 1740 [NLW MS.6376E].
Wrexham, Holt, Gresford, 1738-41 [NLW MS.6393E].
Nanheudwy div. (various townships), 1830-38
  [Longueville Deeds and Documents, 1027].
Colwyn Bay area, 17 parishes, 1946-49 [Inland
  Revenue deposit].

Public Record Office, Kew:
Whole *County*, 1798 [IR.23/116] (see page 9).

Window Tax

Denbighshire Record Office, Ruthin:
Ruthin (Borough), 1770-80 [PD/90/1/178,179].

FLINTSHIRE

Land Tax

Flintshire Record Office, Hawarden:

The only locally held official series of LTAs to
survive are C20.

Divisions
Coleshill: 1936-52, SP.
Maelor: 1936-49, NC
Mold: 1914-28 SP; 1937-8, 1946-9, NC.
Prestatyn: 1933-42, NC.
Rhuddlan: 1933-42, NC.

Survivals for other years as follows: Bagillt, Brynford
  and Greenfield: 1) 1758 [D/DM/114/1-3];
Halghton: 1) 1742-43, 1746-48 [D/LK/20,21,23-25];
Hawarden: 1) 1747 [D/BJ/B9];
Northop: 1) 1732 [P/45/1/381].
Penley: 1) 1746-48 [D/:K/27,29,30];
  3) 1887 [D/KT/57].

National Library of Wales, Aberystwyth:
Cilcain, 1799 [NLW MS.8939 B].
Halkin, Holywell, and Kilken parishes, Greenfield,
  Llysdanhynedd, Soughton and Tre Mostyn
  townships, 1838 [Oldfield Family Papers].

Public Record Office, Kew:
Unaccountably there is no Flintshire volume in
IR.23 (see page 9). In its absence, IR.22/195,
Parish Book of Redemptions, provides some
information.

Window Tax

Flintshire Record Office, Hawarden:

Halghton, 1742, 1745 [D/LK/19,22].
Penley, 1745-47 [D/LK/26,26B,28].
Whitford, 1702-3 [D/NA/1075].

LTA = Land Tax Assessment; M = Many; NC = Near Complete; P = Parishes; S = Some; Y = Years

GLAMORGAN

Land Tax

Glamorgan Archive Service, Cardiff:

1) **Pre-1780:** *Llangyfelach* only 1772-9; Swansea (hundred and town) 1766-7, 1771-9; otherwise isolated LTAs only.
2) **1780-1832:** 1781-1831 good coverage, except Cardiff. Arranged by year, within each hundred. TS list shows exact years for each constablery.
3) **Post-1832:** from 1870 for *Newcastle* and *Ogmore*, otherwise C20 only.

Hundred or Division
Caerphilly: 2) 1783-96, 1800-6, 1808-31, NC.
  3) 1936-49, NC.
Cowbridge: 1) Cowbridge borough only, 1773 [among borough records].
  2) 1783-1831, NC.
  3) 1933-6, 1938-48, NC.
Dinas Powis: 2) 1784-1821, 1823-31, NC.
  3) 1925, 1927-41, 1943-8, NC.
Kibbor: 2) 1782-6, 1788-1806, 1808-31, NC.
  3) 1912, 1914-9, 1928, 1930, 1935-41, 1943-8, NC.
Llangyfelach: 1) 1772-4, 1776-9, NC.
  2) 1781-1806, 1808-21, 1823-31, NC.
Miskin: 2) 1768, 1782-1803, 1805-6, 1808-1831 NC.
  3) 1936-49, NC.
Neath: 2) 1784-90, 1792-1806, 1808-31, NC.
Newcastle: 1) Bettws and Llangynwyd, 1704 [Penrice MSS D/D 908.909].
  2) 1782-1806, 1807-31, NC.
  3) 1870-3, 1875, 1879-82, 1887, 1889-1910, 1912-922, 1925, 1928, 1930, 1933-6. 1938-1948, NC.
Ogmore: 1) 1766-7, NC; Llandyfodwg, 1707 [Blandy Jenkins MSS D/D BJ 0/98].
  2) 1782-1806, 1808-23, 1825-31, NC.
  3) 1870-3, 1875, 1879-82, 1885-6, 1890-5, 1897-1910, 1912-4, 1917, 1933-6, 1938-48, NC.
Swansea (hundred): 1) 1766-7, 1771-9, NC.
  2) 1781-1831, NC.
Cardiff (town): 2) 1788, 1806, 1808, 1819-1821, 1829-30, NC.
Swansea (town): 1) 1766-7, 1773, 1775, 1778, NC.
  2) 1781-1813, 1815-31, NC.
Newport (Hd., co .Mon.): 3) 1911-22, 1925, 1927-1931, 1935-7, 1939-40, 1943-9, SP.

National Library of Wales, Aberystwyth:
1) Swanzey hd., various townships, 1692-3 [Mayberry Collection, 5238].
  1763-68, Eglwsilan, Gellygare, Lanvabon, Rudry [Tredegar Pk MSS 85].
2) Swansea, 1788 [Llangibby Castle D&D, A389].
  Cardiff, St John & St Mary, 1788-1808 [NLW MS. 17796D, typescript books].
3) Baglan, 1862-3 [David & David Val'ns, DD14].
  Cysyllte (Lantrissent, Miskin hd.), 1862-3 [Cilybebyll Deeds, 1375].

West Glamorgan Archive Service, Cardiff:
Hundreds within West Glamorgan availaible on microfilm.

Public Record Office, Kew:
Whole *County,* 1798 [IR.23/117] (see page 9).

Window Tax

Glamorgan Archive Service, Cardiff:

Caerphilly Hundred: 1786, 1795 [WTA/CAE, MTA/CAE].
Cowbridge (Borough), 1773 [B/Cow 179/1-3].

Parishes:
Cadoxton, 1788-90; Glyncorrwg, 1792-3, 1800, and Baglan, 1810 [WTA/N and CTA/N].
Llansannor and Pendoylan, 1783; Llanharan, Llanharry, Llanilid, Pendoylan, Welsh St. Donats, and Ystradowain, 1791 [WTA/COW].

Local Studies Section, South Glamorgan County Library, Cardiff:
Cardiff *(town),* 1769, 1776, 1778, 1780, 1785 [Bute XXV/34/2-8. Catalogue at *Glamorgan Archive Service*].

MERIONETH

Land Tax

Dolgellau Record Office, Dolgellau:

The only locally held LTAs to survive are post-1832.

1862: Dolgellau parish only.
1910, 1930s-40s: whole *County.*

National Library of Wales, Aberystwyth:
Towyn, 1836 (particulars of LTA) [NLW MS. 555B].

Public Record Office, Kew:
Whole *County,* 1798 [IR.23/118] (see page 9).

Window Tax

None located.

Monmouthshire - see with 'England', page 43.

LTA = Land Tax Assessment; M = Many; NC = Near Complete; P = Parishes; S = Some; Y = Years

MONTGOMERYSHIRE

Land Tax

National Library of Wales, Aberystwyth:

1) **Pre-1780:** 1765, 1771-4 most of *County;*
1773 *Hundred of Deuddwr* (list of persons
assessed to LT);
1774 (Canvass Book for whole *County,* showing
how electors are assessed) [all in Powis Castle
Deeds and Documents];
1710, parish of Churchstoke;
1762-79, parish of Berriew [both in Glansevern
Collection].

2) **1780-1832:** much of *County* for 1803, 1805
[Powis Deeds and Documents];
and 1826-31 [Powysland Clubs Collection].

Hundreds
*Pool, Montgomery Lower, Carse Lower, Llanfyllin,
Deuddwr, Pool Lower:* 1825
[Cefnbryntalch Collection].
Berriew (parish), 1780-83 [Glansevern Collection].
Llanfair Caereinion, 1796 [Harrison D&D, 12/10].

3) **Post-1832:** Bodaioch, 1860-1 [Trefeglwys and
Llangurig School & Poor Law Records, B70].
Llandysilio, 1909-10 [NLW ex 1695].
Llandrinio (Deuddwr div.) 1909-10 [NLW Minor
Deposit 1412A].

Powys County Archives Office, *Llandrindod Wells:*

Montgomery Upper, 1792; Machynlleth 1794
[MQS/RE1].

Public Record Office, *Kew:*
Whole *County,* 1798 [IR.23/119] (see page 9).

Window Tax

National Library of Wales, Aberystwyth:

Berriew (parish), 1762-83
[Glansevern Mss. 11856-68].

PEMBROKESHIRE

Land Tax

Published: *Land Tax, Castlemartin Hundred, 1791/2,*
published 1992 by Basil Hughes, 37 Owen Street,
Penner, Pembroke Dock SA72 6SL, £5.50.

Pembrokeshire Record Office, *Haverfordwest:*

1) **Pre-1780:** Haverfordwest, 1698-1721.
2) **1780-1832:** 1786-1831, good survival.
3) **Post-1832:** virtually none.

LTAs are arranged by year.

Hundreds
Castlemartin: 2) 1786-8, 1790-1, 1793-4, 1797,
1801-31, NC. 1791 published.
3) 1931-49, NC.
Cemaes (Kemes): 2) 1786-8, 1790-1, 1793-4, 1796,
1797, 1801-12, 1814-31, NC.
Cilgerran (Kilgerran): 2) as for *Cemaes.*
Dewisland: 2) 1786-8, 1790-1, 1793-4, 1796-7,
1801-31, NC.
Dungleddy: 2) 1786-8, 1790-1, 1793-4, 1796-1797,
1801-28, 1830-1, NC.
Narberth: 2) 1786-8, 1790-1, 1793-4, 1796-7, 1801-
1831, NC (for *Tenby Borough* see below).
3) 1857, 1867-75, 1878-93, 1924-29, NC.
Roose: 2) as for *Narberth.*
3) 1856, parishes of Dale, Haroldston, St. Issells
and Marloes.
Haverfordwest: 1) 1698-1721.
2) 1802, 1806-7, 1810, 1815, 1819, 1823. All
parishes [in HQ/RT - Quarter Sessions -
Haverfordwest].

Tenby Museum, *Tenby:*
Tenby Borough: 2) 1786-1831.

National Library of Wales, Aberystwyth:
Meline, 1703 [Bronwydd Deeds & Documents, 359].
Haverfordwest: St Martyn's, Bridgestreet and
Shipstreet ward, 1719 [NLW MS. 12167E].
Llanychar, 1831-6 [Trenewydd D&D, 199, 201-2].
St Dogwell's, 18857 [Lucas Mss and Records, 734].

Public Record Office, *Kew:*
Whole *County,* 1798 [IR.23/120] (see page 9).

Window Tax

Pembrokeshire Record Office, *Haverfordwest:*
Haverfordwest St Mary's, 1707.

LTA = Land Tax Assessment; M = Many; NC = Near Complete; P = Parishes; S = Some; Y = Years

RADNORSHIRE

Land Tax

Powys County Record Office, Llandrindod Wells:
2) **1780-1832:** 1812-17, 1821-31 whole *County* [Quarter Sessions records].

National Library of Wales, Aberystwyth:
1 & 2). **Pre-1831:** Diserth, 1774-82 [D.T.M. Jones Collection, 1560-2].

3) **Post-1832:** 1846-1943 (with gaps): 31 parishes [Inland Revenue deposit from Hereford].

Public Record Office, Kew:
Whole *County*, 1798 [IR.23/121] (see page 9).

Window Tax

None located.

Hundreds comprising Welsh Counties

Anglesey
1. Talybolion
2. Twrcelyn
3. Llifon
4. Tyndaethwy
5. Malltraeth
6. Menai

Breconshire
7. Builth
8. Merthyr
9. Talgarth
10. Devynnock
11. Penkelly
12. Crickhowell

Caernarvonshire
13. Llysfaen and Errias
14. Creuddyn
15. Isaf
16. Nant-Conwy
17. Uchaf
18. Isgwyrfai
19. Uwchgwyrfai
20. Eifonydd
21. Dinllaen
22. Cafflogion
23. Cymdmaen

Cardiganshire
24. Genau'r Glyn
25. Ilar
26. Penarth
27. Moyddyn
28. Troedyraur

Carmarthenshire
29. Perfedd
30. Caeo/Cayo
31. Catheinog
32. Elvet
33. Derllys
34. Kidwelly
35. Iscennen
36. Carnwallon

Denbighshire
37. Isdulas
38. Isaled
39. Rhuthin/Ruthin
40. Ial/Yale
41. Maelor Bromfield
42. Chirk

Flintshire
43. Prestatyn
44. Rhuddlan
45. Coleshill
46. Mold
47. Maelor

Glamorgan
48. Swansea
49. Llangyfelach
50. Neath
51. Miskin
52. Caerphilly
53. Newcastle
54. Ogmore
55. Cowbridge
56. Dinas Powis
57. Kibbor

Merioneth
58. Edeyrnion
59. Penllyn
60. Ardudwy uwch Artro
61. Ardudwy is Artro
62. Talpont
63. Mawddwy
64. Ystumanner Estimaner

Montgomeryshire
65. Mechain Llanfyllin
66. Caereinion Mathrafel
67. Cyfeiliog Machynlleth
68. Arwystli Llanidloes
69. Cedwain Newtown
70. Ceri/Keri
71. Ystrad Marchell: Pool
72. Y.M.: Deuddwr/Deythur
73. Y.M.: Cawrse
74. Montgomery

Pembrokeshire
75. Cilgerran
76. Cemais
77. Dewsland
78. Dungleddy
79. Rhos
80. Narberth
81. Castlemartin

Radnorshire
82. Rhaeadr
83. Knighton
84. Cefnllys
85. Radnor
86. Colwyn
87. Painscastle